A JOYFUL NOISE

A JOYFUL NOISE

Praying the Psalms with the Early Church

MIKE AQUILINA

Foreword by Scott Hahn

EMMAUS ROAD
PUBLISHING

www.EmmausRoad.org
Steubenville, Ohio

Emmaus Road Publishing
1468 Parkview Circle
Steubenville, Ohio 43952

© 2017 Mike Aquilina
All rights reserved. Second edition 2017 by Emmaus Road Publishing.
First edition 2009 by The Word Among Us Press.
Printed in the United States of America

Library of Congress Cataloging-in-Publication Data:
Names: Aquilina, Mike, author.
Title: A joyful noise : praying the Psalms with the early Church / Mike Aquilina.
Other titles: Praying the Psalms with the early Christians
Description: Second edition. | Steubenville : Emmaus Road, 2017. |
 Identifiers: LCCN 2017041837 (print) | LCCN 2017043098 (ebook) | ISBN 9781947792319 (ebook) | ISBN 9781947792296 (hard cover) | ISBN 9781947792302 (pbk.)
Subjects: LCSH: Bible. Psalms--Devotional use. | Bible. Psalms--Criticism, interpretation, etc.
Classification: LCC BS1430.54 (ebook) | LCC BS1430.54 .A68 2017 (print) | DDC 264/.02015--dc23
LC record available at https://lccn.loc.gov/2017041837

Unless otherwise noted, Scripture quotations are taken from The Revised Standard Version Second Catholic Edition (Ignatius Edition) Copyright © 2006 by the Division of Christian Education of the National Council of the Churches of Christ in the United States of America. Used by permission. All rights reserved.

Excerpts from the Catechism of the Catholic Church, second edition, copyright © 2000, Libreria Editrice Vaticana—United States Conference of Catholic Bishops, Washington, D.C.

Cover image: *Concerto degli Angeli* (ca. 1534–1536) by Gaudenzio Ferrari, Santuario della Madonna dei Miracoli, Saronno, Italy / Wikimedia Commons

Cover design and layout by Margaret Ryland

For Isabella Maria

Contents

Foreword by Scott Hahn	ix
Introduction: Music for Our Hearts	xiii
The Early Christians on the Psalms	xix
Psalm 1	1
Psalm 2	7
Psalm 4	13
Psalm 9	17
Psalm 12	21
Psalm 15	25
Psalm 19	27
Psalm 22	31
Psalm 23	37
Psalm 27	41
Psalm 29	47
Psalm 32	51
Psalm 34	55
Psalm 40	61
Psalm 42	67
Psalm 45	73
Psalm 51	77
Psalm 53	83
Psalm 54	89

Psalm 58	93
Psalm 67	97
Psalm 70	101
Psalm 73	107
Psalm 78	113
Psalm 82	121
Psalm 85	125
Psalm 94	131
Psalm 100	137
Psalm 102	141
Psalm 104	147
Psalm 110	153
Psalm 118	159
Psalm 121	163
Psalm 127	167
Psalm 131	171
Psalm 134	177
Psalm 137	181
Psalm 141	185
Psalm 145	189
About the Fathers	193
Sources	213

Foreword

Of all the books of the Bible, the most beloved are the Gospels and the Psalms. Christians share a nature that is common to all humanity, and it is naturally human to love stories and songs. In the Gospels and the Psalms, grace builds on nature, completes it, elevates it, and fulfills it.

It seems that the early Christians even favored the songs over the stories. There are more ancient commentaries on the Psalms than on any other book of the Bible, and the nearest contenders are pretty far behind. There are good natural reasons for this trend (which continued long into the Middle Ages). The Psalms have the advantage of melody, which makes them memorable and easily memorizable. They have the further advantage of poetic techniques, like repeated refrains and parallelism, which play to all the weaknesses and strengths of the mind and heart.

Still in the natural order, most of the Psalms have the advantage of authorship by a consummate artist—a genius on the order of Homer, Vergil, and Dante. That poet, furthermore, enjoyed the assistance of almighty God as he set down his verses. That detail moves us beyond the order of nature, however, and into the supernatural. The Psalms are masterworks not only of nature, but also of grace.

And so we Catholics have always sung them with gusto. The Church has always been (to borrow a phrase from James Joyce) "Here Comes Everybody." Not everyone can read. Not everyone wants to blather and ponder texts in a classroom or Bible study. But we can all grieve. We can all delight. We are all moved to affections that are most difficult to express.

One of the early Fathers, Saint John Cassian compared Christians to hedgehogs. We range and graze freely and openly in the pasture of the Psalms. Each believer, he said, will begin to sing the Psalms "in such a way that he will utter them with the deepest emotion of heart not as if they were the compositions of the Psalmist, but rather as if they were his own utterances and his very own prayer."

The Psalms are the Scriptures, he added, that are immediately relevant, immediately convicting, immediately our own—like a popular song that has stayed with us from childhood and can still move us to tears. Yet the Psalms are so much more powerful because God is their co-author—and he is our co-author as well.

In the Psalms, "the Holy Scriptures lie open to us . . . as if their very veins and marrow are exposed. Our experience not only perceives but actually anticipates their meaning, and the sense of the words is revealed to us, not by an exposition of them, but by practical proof." Isn't this the way the Psalms affect us today?

Certainly. That's why they remain, to this day, the only biblical book that we sing or recite at every single Mass. To sing is to pray twice. To sing the Psalms is to raise an unerring and infallible prayer to God.

Some people will wonder why all this is so. The Psalms, after all, were written a thousand years before the Lord's Incarnation. Why should they be singled out in this way?

Saint Augustine, more than anyone, appreciated the special place of the Psalms in Christian life. They are not deficient because they preceded the earthly life of Christ. Indeed, they are often cited in proofs of Jesus' divinity. In hundreds of ways, in thousands of verses, they anticipated his saving work. The New Testament, Augustine taught, is concealed in the Old, and the Old is revealed in the New. The Psalms, he said, are (mystically) the words of Christ and words about Christ.

This is the common doctrine of the Fathers. In these pages we pray and sing along with Saint Hippolytus of Rome, Saint Athanasius of Alexandria, Saint Hilary of Poitiers, Saint John Chrysostom, Saint Basil of Caesarea, Saint Cyril of Jerusalem, and so many others. How's that for catholicity? These early Christians lived in lands far-flung, and they differed in the languages they used to sing the Psalms. Yet they sang—and they still sing with us—with one voice.

—Scott Hahn
Professor of Theology,
Franciscan University of Steubenville

Introduction

Music for Our Hearts

Turn off the television.
Turn off the radio.
Turn off the computer.
Go to the quietest room in the house.
Shut the door.
Sit down and close your eyes.

You can still hear it, can't you? The irritating car dealer commercial, the endless loop of background music in the computer game, the dopey dialogue from that stupid movie that you never would have watched if anything half-decent had been on.

And every fleeting thought sets off some song in your head—a song you can't silence, no matter how hard you try, especially if it's a song you hate.

It would be nice if we could set aside some time for meditation and prayer. But who can meditate with all that racket going on?

But if we take our own racket with us even into our quiet spots, what can we do? How can we escape? How can we devote our minds to spiritual things instead of the world's constant parade of temptations and trivia?

Maybe we can't escape the racket. But there's no reason we can't change it. We might even make our constant mental soundtrack work *for* us instead of *against* us, pushing us toward spiritual things instead of dragging us away.

This is exactly the advice the early Christians got from the best thinkers of the age. After all, their world was not so different from ours. Wherever Christians went, they heard music—then as much as now. It stuck in their heads and invaded their thoughts, just the way it does to us.

St. John Chrysostom said

> So much does our nature take pleasure in chants and songs that even babies at the breast, when they are weeping and troubled, are lulled to sleep. For the same reason, travelers sing at mid-day as they drive their yoked animals, and thus they ease by song the hardships of the journey. And not only travelers, but laborers, too, often sing as they tread the grapes in the winepress, gather the harvest, dress the vines, and do their other jobs. Sailors do the same, rowing the oars. And women sing a certain melody as they weave and sort the tangled threads... Women, travelers, workers, and sailors, try to ease with a chant the hardship that goes with their toil, for the mind endures hardships and difficulties more readily when it hears songs and chants.
>
> —*Exposition of Psalm 41*

Make a Joyful Noise

Music is the natural accompaniment to our lives, as St. John Chrysostom points out. We are human; our lives move to music and song. But *what* music and *what* song? Those are the important questions.

Egeria, a woman of the 300s who wrote a famous memoir of her pilgrimage to the Holy Land with an early group of Christian tourists, tells us that they sang psalms wherever they went:

For it was always customary with us that, whenever we succeeded in reaching the places we desired to visit, prayer should first be made there, then the lection should be read from the book, then one appropriate psalm should be said, then prayer should be made again. At God's bidding we always kept to this custom, whenever we were able to come to the places we desired.

—The Pilgrimage of Etheria

Just like the laborers in the fields, the seamstresses at their sewing, and the sailors on the sea, these Christian pilgrims made music wherever they went. But the music they chose was the psalms. Everywhere they went, Christians made the psalms their soundtrack. They learned to love these sacred songs in the same way teenagers today love their favorite bands.

Not long ago, archaeologists in Egypt found the mummified body of a fifth-century Christian boy buried with his greatest treasures in his hands: a Coptic cross and a Book of Psalms.

Today, Christians everywhere love the Cross. But how many of us know and love the psalms as well as that ancient Egyptian boy?

Sing a New Song

The Book of Psalms has been the prayer book and the hymnal of God's people for three thousand years. Israel sang the psalms of David in the Temple built by the son of David.

When the Messiah came, however, the Church sang the Psalter as a "new song to the Lord" (see, among others, Psalm 96:1). In every psalm they saw a startlingly clear expression of the love they felt for Christ—the love that burned so bright that they were willing to die for it if that was what Christ called them to do.

In the years and the centuries after Pentecost, Christians came to see the psalms as the preeminent prayers of the New Covenant. And the saints of the Early Church came to see Christ at the center of the psalms.

The psalms were the prayers *of Christ*.

They were prayers *to Christ*.

And they were prayers *about Christ*.

So the psalms rang out in the worship of the Early Church. They're everywhere in the ancient rituals. Even today, the Book of Psalms is the one book of the Bible that is read at just about every Mass.

But the psalms were more than just set pieces in the liturgy. In the preaching of the holy Fathers—Chrysostom, Augustine, and Basil—the psalms were the very voice of Christ, raised through the ages in his body, the Church.

The monks of the Egyptian desert prayed all the psalms every single day. (Monks everywhere still do.) In the lives of early Christian women like Egeria, the psalms were sacred touchstones of everyday life. There was an appropriate psalm for every occasion.

Those early saints remain with us as a "great cloud of witnesses" (Hebrews 12:1). This book brings their words and liturgies together, so that we might raise our voices with theirs and sing the psalms again as a "new song"—and so that we might sing with one voice, the voice of Christ.

We're also trying to start a good habit. It's a good thing if a psalm comes spontaneously to our lips in times of joy or sorrow. But a psalm is more likely to arise if we have made a habit of praying the psalms—as the early Christians did—with regularity, in season and out of season. At Mass and at designated hours day and night, the Church prayed (and prays) specific psalms in their endless rounds, whether the members of the congregation "feel" like this or that particular psalm or not. We are sowing songs in the heart for their harvest in due season.

How to Use This Book

You'll find thirty-five psalms within these pages. Including all 150 psalms would have made the book far too long. But don't assume that these are the best psalms—they're just the ones I have chosen. You'll enjoy exploring the rest of the psalms on your own, especially once you pick up on the reading methods of the Church Fathers.

Each psalm has a brief introduction that puts it in context.

After the text of the psalm, I've selected some "words to remember"—just a few lines you can repeat to yourself on and off throughout the day. There was a time when it was common to memorize whole psalms. (The Council of Nicaea decreed that every bishop should know the Psalter by heart!) But even just a snatch of one of these sacred songs is a good thing to carry with you.

Next come a few words from one or two great early Christian thinkers.

Finally, a couple of "questions to think about" will help you apply the words of the psalm, and the ideas of the early Christians, to your own spiritual life.

The back section contains short biographies of all the Christian writers in this book. Knowing something about their lives sometimes gives us even more insight into what they had to say about the psalms and why they said it. And beyond that, it's a real privilege to meet these heroes of the faith, who can serve as examples for us to imitate.

The pages at the very end of the book provide a list of sources where you'll find the Fathers' meditations in full, in their original context.

Remember: the purpose of this book is to help you draw closer to God, to speak with him intimately, to listen to him, to rest in him. That, after all, is the reason why God inspired the psalms. They are songs of the heart—sometimes expressing the depths of his Sacred Heart, sometimes expressing the failings of our very human hearts. And they are timeless—ancient songs that still speak to our modern hearts.

I hope that some of the greatest saints of the Christian tradition will help you to pray the psalms—not just to read them or recite them, but to make them part of your life. Every human emotion is expressed in the psalms, and expressed more beautifully than almost anywhere else in literature. What better way to draw closer to God in prayer than by finding the psalm that tells him just how you feel?

An added benefit is that you'll meet many of the earliest Christian thinkers and saints, men and women who helped shape our Christian faith. And since, for them, the psalms were all about Christ, I hope that ultimately this book will bring you closer to Jesus.

—Mike Aquilina

The Early Christians on the Psalms

For the early Christians, the psalms were staples of ritual worship and were regularly recited and sung in the daily rounds of the monasteries. Many of the Fathers read the psalms, like much of the Old Testament, as prefiguring the life of Christ and the life of Christians in the Church.

Of course the psalmists—King David and others—were unaware of these things. Our Lord's Incarnation was still centuries away. But the Early Church, using analogy, discerned a Christian meaning in the psalms. For the Apostles and for the Fathers, the Bible was a book about Christ, a single story of God's revelation to mankind, a story that culminates in the Incarnation, when the Word became flesh. The biblical events were historical, but they took on a universal significance as they were fulfilled in Christ. And so the early Christians drew out—in addition to the literal and historical meaning of the psalms—Christological, moral, and heavenly meanings as well. St. Paul refers to this method as "allegory" (Galatians 4:24) as he applies it to the story of Sarah and Hagar in the Book of Genesis. An allegory is a story that serves as an extended metaphor, in which characters and other details are equated with the meanings that lie outside the narrative. Thus, an allegory is a story with at least two levels of meaning: one literal and the other symbolic.

Subsequent generations followed the Apostle in reading the Scriptures allegorically. In the pages to come, we will encounter this method quite often. St. Augustine, for example, sees the infant and adult Babylonians in Psalm 137 as an allegory for venial and mortal sin.

Allegory is the way the Church Fathers applied the Scriptures to life as it was lived centuries or millennia after the historical events that had been recorded in the Bible. Allegory does not deny the truth of the historical event, but rather acknowledges its applicability for all people and all time. Moreover, with God as its primary author, the scriptural text held meanings that its human authors and their contemporaries could not even begin to fathom—meanings that would become apparent only when viewed through their eventual fulfillment in Jesus Christ.

As we read the Fathers, we see that the Church has always drawn from the psalms to enrich our understanding of Christian doctrines—from the nature of the Trinity, to the efficacy of the sacraments, to the gift of purgatory.

Let us join the Fathers and our forerunners in the Faith in plumbing the depths of the psalms and discovering the richness hidden within them.

Sing with the Heart

It's not how well you sing that matters, says St. Jerome, who himself translated the psalms from the original Hebrew. The thing that matters is the heart.

> "Addressing one another in psalms and hymns and spiritual songs, singing and making melody to the Lord with all your heart" (Ephesians 5:19).
>
> If you are not debauched with drunkenness, and

by keeping from it are full of the Spirit, then you are ready for everything: psalms, hymns, and songs. We can learn from the Book of Psalms how the psalm, hymn, and song are different. Here let us just say that hymns proclaim the Lord's might and majesty, and praise his works and his benefits constantly. The psalms that begin or end with the word "Alleluia" are all hymns. In addition, psalms specifically affect the conscience, so that we can know by means of it what we should and should not do. Songs are more philosophical, looking into the order of the universe and how all created things work together in it.

To put it in simpler terms, a psalm aims for the body, a song aims for the mind. So we should sing, make music, and praise the Lord with the heart more than the voice.

And this is just what Scripture tells us: "singing and making melody to the Lord with all your heart." Young people should hear this. Those who make music in church should hear this. Don't sing to God with the voice: sing to God with the heart. Don't wax your throat like a popular actor, so that you turn the church into a music hall. Sing in fear of God, with care, and knowing the Scriptures.

Even if you're tone deaf... if your works are good, your song is sweet to God. If you would serve Christ, don't worry about your voice, but concentrate on the good words you sing, to make sure the evil spirit that attacked Saul (see 1 Samuel 16:14–23) will not come into those who would make a music hall out of the Church.

—St. Jerome, *Commentary on Ephesians*

One Occasion for Tears

When his sister, a saintly abbess, died, St. Gregory of Nyssa mourned as inconsolably as everyone else. And then, as he recalled it later, he thought of what his sister would tell him. If we must weep, let us remember a psalm to weep with.

> But when, as if from sleep, I recovered my thoughts, I looked toward that holy face and it seemed as if it rebuked me for the confusion of the noisy mourners. So I called to the sisters with a loud voice:
> "Look at her, and remember her commands, by which she trained you to be orderly and decent in everything. One occasion for tears did this divine soul ordain for us, recommending us to weep at the time of prayer. Which now we may do, by turning the lamentations into psalmody in the same strain."
>
> —St. Gregory of Nyssa, *Life of St. Macrina*

Everything Is in the Psalms

St. Athanasius, the great champion of true doctrine, sees in the psalms a little bit of everything that's in all the other books of Scripture: history, law, prophecy, and even the Gospel.

> Son, all the books of Scripture, both Old Testament and New, are inspired by God and useful for instruction, as the Apostle says (2 Timothy 3:16); but to those who really study it the Psalter yields special treasure. ... For I think that in the words of this book all human life is covered, with all its states and thoughts, and that nothing further can be found in man. For no

matter what you seek, whether it be repentance and confession, or help in trouble and temptation or under persecution, whether you have been set free from plots and snares or, on the contrary, are sad for any reason, or whether, seeing yourself progressing and your enemy cast down, you want to praise and thank and bless the Lord, each of these things the divine psalms show you how to do, and in every case the words you want are written down for you, and you can say them as your own.

—St. Athanasius, *Letter to Marcellinus*

Psalm 1

A bit of wisdom is a fitting beginning to the Book of Psalms. Psalm 1 contrasts the wise and good, whose "delight is in the law of the Lord," with the wicked and foolish, in whom nothing is permanent.

> Blessed is the man
>   who walks not in the counsel of the wicked,
> nor stands in the way of sinners,
>   nor sits in the seat of scoffers;
> but his delight is in the law of the Lord,
>   and on his law he meditates day and night.
> He is like a tree
>   planted by streams of water,
> that yields its fruit in its season,
>   and its leaf does not wither.
> In all that he does, he prospers.
>
> The wicked are not so,
>   but are like chaff which the wind drives away.
> Therefore the wicked will not stand in the judgment,
>   nor sinners in the congregation of the righteous;
> for the Lord knows the way of the righteous,
>   but the way of the wicked will perish.

> **Words to Remember**
> ... his delight is in the law of the Lord,
>   and on his law he meditates day and night.

Begin with an End in Mind

Every part of Scripture has something in particular to teach us, says St. Basil the Great, but the Book of Psalms contains all this wisdom in one place. Because it's hard to get the true doctrine through to us, the Holy Spirit set the truth to music so that we could learn while we enjoyed the singing. In this first psalm, David shows us where we'll be going so that we'll know that the journey is worthwhile.

> All Scripture is inspired by God and useful (2 Timothy 3:16) and was composed by the Holy Spirit. It's like a general hospital for souls, where all people may choose the right medicine for their own diseases. . . . The prophets teach certain things, the histories others, the Law still others, and the sort of counsel given in Proverbs others.
>
> But the Book of the Psalms holds whatever is helpful in all the others. It foretells things to come. It recalls past history. It gives laws for life. It gives advice about what to do. It is a storehouse of good instructions, carefully giving what is useful to each.
>
> It gives healing to the ancient wounds of souls and speedy remedy to fresh wounds. It cares for the sick and keeps the healthy. It removes the agitations—no matter how great and no matter what kind—that dominate the soul in our lifetime. And it does this through timely persuasion that inspires sound thinking.
>
> The Holy Spirit saw that humanity had only weak inclinations toward virtue and that we were ignorant of the righteous life because of our preference for pleasure. So what did he do? He combined the delight of melody with doctrines, so that through pleasing

and soft sound we might receive, without noticing, what was useful in the words. When wise physicians give bitter potions to the sick, they often smear the rim of the cup with honey. In a similar way, the beautiful melodies of the psalms have been designed for us, so that those who are young, or young at heart, may truly educate their souls while they appear to be singing. For hardly anyone in the lazy crowds goes [home from church] with a memory of any precept of the apostles or prophets—but the words of the psalms they sing at home and spread in the marketplace. And if someone who suffers from excessive and beastly anger falls under the spell of a psalm, he leaves [church] with the ferocity of his soul calmed by the melody.

A psalm is serenity for the soul, the bringer of peace, restraining the disorder and tumult of thoughts. It softens the agitation of the soul and disciplines its rebelliousness. A psalm forms friendships, unites those who are divided, reconciles enemies. Who can still consider someone an enemy when they have sung together to God? So the singing of psalms brings love, the greatest of good things. Harmony becomes the bond of unity for people who sing together in a choir. . . .

To the soldiers of true religion, David set out to propose many arduous tasks, requiring hard sweat and labor. But first he showed the happy goal, so that with the hope of blessings to come we might endure the sufferings of this life without grief. The hope of comfortable lodging eases the journey of travelers on a rough road. The desire for goods makes merchants brave the ocean. The promise of the crop removes the drudgery from the work of farmers. Just so, the one who orders all our lives, the great teacher, the Spirit of truth, wisely set before us the rewards, so that we might rise above the work at hand and persevere in spirit till we enjoy the everlasting blessings.

"Blessed is the man who walks not in the counsel of the wicked." What is truly good, then, is first and foremost the most blessed; and that is God. So Paul, too, discusses Christ: "awaiting our blessed hope, the appearing of the glory of our great God and Savior Jesus Christ" (Titus 2:13). For truly blessed is the goodness that all things await and all things desire: an unchangeable nature, noble dignity, peaceful existence, a happy way of life in which there is neither change nor alteration. . . .

But foolish and worldly men, ignorant of the nature of good itself, often bless what is worthless: wealth, health, and fame. None of these is good by nature, and not only because they easily change to their opposite, but also because they cannot make their owners good. Who is just because of what he owns? Who is self-possessed because of his health? Quite the contrary: each of these things easily becomes the servant of sin for those who use them wrongly. Blessed is he, then, who has what is valued the most: who shares in goods that cannot be lost. How do we know him? He "walks not in the counsel of the wicked." . . .

But why, you may ask, does the prophet single out "man" for happiness? Are women excluded? No! For the virtue of man and woman is the same, since creation is equally honored in both; and so both receive the same reward. Listen to Genesis: "God created man in his own image, in the image of God he created him; male and female he created them" (Genesis 1:27). Those whose nature is alike share the same reward.

So why did Scripture mention man, but not woman? Because their nature is alike to indicate the whole through the part, and that is sufficient.

—St. Basil the Great, *Homily on Psalm 1*

> **Questions to Think About**
> 1. How well do I value, first and foremost, the things that are everlasting?
> 2. How do I define happiness? Blessedness? Fulfillment?
> 3. How can I make the psalms in particular, and the Bible in general, a bigger part of my life?

Psalm 2

Psalm 2 is one of the famous messianic psalms—that is, the psalms that are most often taken by Christians as referring to Jesus Christ. When it was written, this psalm did, of course, refer to the earthly king of Israel. But the words "You are my son, today I have begotten you" are cited several times in the New Testament (Acts 13:33; Hebrews 1:5 and 5:5) to show that Jesus is the true eternal King of Israel.

Why do the nations conspire,
    and the peoples plot in vain?
The kings of the earth set themselves,
    and the rulers take counsel together,
    against the Lord and his anointed, saying,
"Let us burst their bonds asunder,
    and cast their cords from us."

He who sits in the heavens laughs;
    the Lord has them in derision.
Then he will speak to them in his wrath,
    and terrify them in his fury, saying,
"I have set my king
    on Zion, my holy hill."

I will tell of the decree of the Lord:
He said to me, "You are my son,
    today I have begotten you.
Ask of me, and I will make the nations your heritage,
    and the ends of the earth your possession.

You shall break them with a rod of iron,
   and dash them in pieces like a potter's vessel."

Now therefore, O kings, be wise;
   be warned, O rulers of the earth.
Serve the Lord with fear,
   with trembling kiss his feet,
lest he be angry, and you perish in the way;
   for his wrath is quickly kindled.

Blessed are all who take refuge in him.

> **Words to Remember**
> I will tell of the decree of the Lord:
> He said to me, "You are my son,
>   today I have begotten you."

God the King and Human Authority

If God is King, how can earthly rulers be "kings"? If Christ is the Son of God, how can human beings be "children of God"? St. Aphrahat tells us that this is not a diminution of God's authority but a manifestation of God's glory. God is so great that he can share with us not only his authority but even his divinity.

➣ God called Israel "my first-born" when he sent Moses to Pharaoh to say, "Israel is my first-born son, and I say to you, 'Let my son go that he may serve me'; if you refuse to let him go, behold, I will slay your first-born son" (Exodus 4:22–23). And he said the same thing through the prophet Hosea (11:1–2), and reproved them and said to the people, "Out of Egypt have I called my son"... And again it is written, "You are the children of the Lord your God" (Deuteronomy 14:1). And about Solomon he said, "He shall be to me a son, and I will be to him a Father" (2 Samuel 8:14).

So we also call Christ the Son of God, for through him we have gained the knowledge of God. In the same way, God called Israel "my firstborn son," and said of Solomon, "He shall be to me a son."... David said about them: "You are gods and children of the Highest, all of you." And when they did not turn away from their sin, he said about them: "As men shall you die, and as one of the princes shall you fall."

For the highest honor in the world is to be called divine, and God applies it to anyone with whom he is well pleased.... For by the mouth of his prophet God called the heathen King Nebuchadnezzar "King of Kings." Jeremiah said: "Every people and kingdom that shall not put his neck into the yoke of Nebuchadnezzar, King of Kings, my servant, with famine and with sword and with pestilence will I visit that people."

Though God is the great King, he does not deny the title of kingship to men. Likewise, though he is the great God, he still did not deny the title of Godhead to the sons of flesh! And though all fatherhood is his, he has also called men fathers. For he said to the congregation: "Instead of your fathers shall be your sons" (Psalm 45:16). And though authority is his, he has given men authority one over another. And while worship is to honor him, he still allows one man to honor another in the world. For even though a man should do worship before the wicked and the heathen and those who refuse grace, he is still not censured by God.

And concerning worship he commanded his people, "You shall not worship the sun or the moon or all the hosts of heaven; and also you shall not desire to worship any creature that is upon the earth" (Deuteronomy 4:17).

See the grace and the love of our good Maker! He did not withhold from men the name of Godhead and the name of worship, and the name of Kingship, and the name of authority; because he is the Father of the created things that are over the face of the world, and he has honored and exalted and glorified men above all creatures. For with his holy hands he fashioned them; and he breathed his Spirit into them, and he became a dwelling-place to them from the beginning. He lives in them and walks among them. For he said through the prophet, "I will dwell in them, and walk in them" (Leviticus 26:12). And the prophet Jeremiah said: "You are the temple of the Lord, if you make fair your ways and your deeds." And long ago David said: "You, Lord, have been a dwelling place unto us for generations; before the mountains were conceived and before the earth travailed, and before the world was framed; from age to age you are God."

—St. Aphrahat, *Demonstration 17*

"Today I Have Begotten You"

What does it mean to say that the Son is begotten "today"? Was the Son of God begotten at a particular point in time? No, answers St. Augustine: "today" means literally "right now," because the Son is eternally begotten of the Father.

> "He said to me, 'You are my son, today I have begotten you.'"

Now, this may seem to be speaking prophetically of that day on which Jesus Christ was born according to the flesh. In eternity there is nothing past as if it had ceased to be, nor future as if it were not yet, but everything is present, since whatever is eternal always is.

Yet since "today" suggests the present, a divine interpretation is given to that expression, "today I have begotten you," by which the uncorrupted and Catholic faith proclaims the eternal generation of the power and Wisdom of God, who is the Only-Begotten Son.

"Ask of me, and I shall give you the nations for your inheritance."

Right away we see a worldly sense here, referring to the manhood which he took on himself—he who offered up himself as a Sacrifice in place of all sacrifices, and who also makes intercession for us. The words "ask of me," then, may refer to this whole world below: ask of me that the nations may be joined to the Name of Christ, and so be redeemed from death, and possessed by God.

"I shall give you the nations for your inheritance": you shall possess them for their salvation, and to bear spiritual fruit for you.

"And the uttermost parts of the earth for your possession."

The same repeated: "the uttermost parts of the earth" is put for "the nations"; but more clearly, so that we might understand all the nations. And "your possession" stands for "your inheritance."

—St. Augustine, *Exposition on the Psalms*

> **Questions to Think About**
> 1. What does it mean for me to exercise kingship?
> 2. For the early Christians, to be "saved" was to be a child of God. Do I understand this as the deepest meaning of salvation?

Psalm 4

This is a hymn of faith. Even when the world dismisses us, and the wicked seem to prosper, we know that God stands by us. That's all we need, because it's more than wealth can buy or power can extort. With God on our side, we can have absolute confidence.

To the choirmaster: with stringed instruments.
A Psalm of David.

Answer me when I call, O God of my right!
   You have given me room when I was in distress.
Be gracious to me, and hear my prayer.

O men, how long will you be dull of heart?
   How long will you love vain words, and seek after
      lies? *Selah*
But know that the LORD has set apart the godly for
   himself;
   the LORD hears when I call to him.

Be angry, but sin not;
   commune with your own hearts on your beds, and
      be silent. *Selah*
Offer right sacrifices,
   and put your trust in the LORD.

There are many who say, "O that we might see some
   good!

Lift up the light of your countenance upon us, O
  Lord!"
you have put more joy in my heart
  than they have when their grain and wine abound.

In peace I will both lie down and sleep;
  for you alone, O Lord, make me dwell in safety.

> **Words to Remember**
> In peace I will both lie down and sleep;
>   for you alone, O Lord, make me dwell in safety.

A Christian Woman's Last Words

At the funeral of his beloved sister, St. Gregory of Nazianzus recalls her last words. To a Christian who made the psalms the rhythm of her life, the words of the psalms came naturally as the most fitting accompaniment to death.

Trembling and tears have seized upon me, at the recollection of the wonder. She was just passing away, and at her last breath, surrounded by a group of relatives and friends performing the last offices of kindness, while her aged mother bent over her, with her soul convulsed with envy of her departure, anguish and affection being blended in the minds of all.

Some longed to hear some burning word to be branded in their recollection; others were eager to speak, yet no one dared; for tears were mute and the pangs of grief unconsoled, since it seemed sacrilegious to think that mourning could be an honor to one who was thus passing away.

So there was solemn silence, as if her death had been a religious ceremony.

There she lay, to all appearance, breathless, motionless, speechless; the stillness of her body seemed paralysis, as though the organs of speech were dead, after that which could move them was gone. But as her pastor, who in this wonderful scene was carefully watching her, perceived that her lips were gently moving, and placed his ear to them, which his disposition and sympathy emboldened him to do...

But you [turning to the pastor] expound the meaning of this mysterious calm, for no one can disbelieve it on your word! Under her breath she was repeating a psalm—the last words of a psalm—to say the truth, a testimony to the boldness with which she was departing. And blessed is he who can fall asleep with these words: "In peace I will both lie down and sleep."

Thus were you singing, fairest of women, and thus it happened to you; and the song became a reality, and attended on thy departure as a memorial of thee, who hast entered upon sweet peace after suffering, and received (over and above the rest which comes to all), that sleep which is due to the beloved, as befitted one who lived and died amid the words of piety.

—St. Gregory of Nazianzus,
Funeral Oration on His Sister Gorgonia

> **Questions to Think About**
> 1. Do I worry about everything? Does that mean I haven't really placed my trust in God?
> 2. How ready am I ready to go home when God calls me?

Psalm 9

A hymn of praise to God for deliverance so far, Psalm 9 is also a plea that the deliverance may continue. The psalm is attributed to David, who certainly had enough occasions in his long conflict with Saul to thank God for saving him, while at the same time realizing that he wasn't out of the woods yet.

To the choirmaster: according to Muth-labben.
A Psalm of David.

I will give thanks to the LORD with my whole heart;
    I will tell of all your wonderful deeds.
I will be glad and exult in you,
    I will sing praise to your name, O Most High.

When my enemies turned back,
    they stumbled and perished before you.
For you have maintained my just cause;
    you have sat on the throne giving righteous
        judgment.

You have rebuked the nations, you have destroyed the
        wicked;
    you have blotted out their name for ever and ever.
The enemy have vanished in everlasting ruins;
    their cities you have rooted out;
    the very memory of them has perished.

But the LORD sits enthroned for ever,
 he has established his throne for judgment;
and he judges the world with righteousness,
 he judges the peoples with equity.

The LORD is a stronghold for the oppressed,
 a stronghold in times of trouble.
And those who know thy name put their trust in you,
 for you, O LORD, have not forsaken those who seek you.

Sing praises to the LORD, who dwells in Zion!
 Tell among the peoples his deeds!
For he who avenges blood is mindful of them;
 he does not forget the cry of the afflicted.

Be gracious to me, O LORD!
 Behold what I suffer from those who hate me,
 O you who lift me up from the gates of death,
that I may recount all your praises,
 that in the gates of the daughter of Zion
 I may rejoice in your deliverance.

The nations have sunk in the pit which they made;
 in the net which they hid has their own foot been caught.
The LORD has made himself known, he has executed judgment;
 the wicked are snared in the work of their own hands. *Higgaion. Selah*

The wicked shall depart to Sheol,
 all the nations that forget God.

For the needy shall not always be forgotten,
 and the hope of the poor shall not perish for ever.

Arise, O LORD! Let not man prevail;
 let the nations be judged before you!
Put them in fear, O LORD!
 Let the nations know that they are but men! *Selah*

> **Words to Remember**
> The LORD is a stronghold for the oppressed,
> a stronghold in times of trouble.
> And those who know your name put their trust in you,
> for you, O LORD, have not forsaken those who seek
> you.

How Anyone Can "Forget" and Still Remember God

St. Augustine explains what it means for nations to have "forgotten" God by giving us a familiar example. We all know what it's like when someone recognizes us right away—even though we have no idea who he is. If he reminds us of the circumstances under which we knew him, suddenly we find that the memory isn't really gone at all. It was still there, somewhere, waiting to be drawn out.

> Somebody you don't recognize says to you, "You know me"; and in order to remind you, tells you where, when, and how you got to know him. And if, after he's told you everything he can think of to make you remember him, you still don't recognize him, then you've forgot-

ten so completely that all that knowledge is altogether blotted out of your mind. There is nothing else for you to do but take his word for it when he tells you that you once knew him—or not even that, if you don't think the person speaking to you can be trusted.

But if you do remember him, then no doubt you return to your own memory, and find that the knowledge had not been altogether blotted out by forgetfulness.

Now, back to the passage that brought up the subject in the first place. Among other things, the ninth psalm says, "The wicked shall depart to Sheol, all the nations that forget God"; and again the twenty-second psalm, "All the ends of the earth shall remember and turn to the Lord."

These nations, then, will not have forgotten God so much that they can't remember him when reminded of him. Yet, by forgetting God, as though forgetting their own life, they had been turned into death; that is, into hell. But when reminded, they turn back to the Lord, as though coming to life again by remembering their real life, which they had forgotten.

—St. Augustine, *On the Holy Trinity*

Questions to Think About
1. How often do I remember to thank God for the safety I have now—even when I'm not out of the woods yet?
2. Why would praise be an appropriate response to God's protection of me? Have I remembered that one of the reasons for God's protection is so that I can praise God to the whole world?

Psalm 12

Here is another prayer to God to rescue the godly from the wicked. This is a psalm to remember when the whole world seems to be out of control: even when "every one utters lies to his neighbor," we know that "the promises of the Lord are promises that are pure."

To the choirmaster: according to The Sheminith.
A Psalm of David.

Help, Lord; for there is no longer any that is godly;
   for the faithful have vanished from among the sons
      of men.
Every one utters lies to his neighbor;
   with flattering lips and a double heart they speak.

May the Lord cut off all flattering lips,
   the tongue that makes great boasts,
those who say, "With our tongue we will prevail,
   our lips are with us; who is our master?"

"Because the poor are despoiled, because the needy
      groan,
   I will now arise," says the Lord;
   "I will place him in the safety for which he longs."
The promises of the Lord are promises that are pure,
   silver refined in a furnace on the ground,
   purified seven times.

Do, O Lord, protect us,
   guard us ever from this generation.
On every side the wicked prowl,
   as vileness is exalted among the sons of men.

> **Words to Remember**
> "Because the poor are despoiled, because the needy
>   groan,
>   I will now arise," says the Lord.

Purified Seven Times

St. Augustine relates the sevenfold purification in the psalm to the Beatitudes in the Sermon on the Mount. Though the righteous are tried by the wicked, God promises them safety in Christ.

> *"Because the poor are despoiled, because the needy groan, I will now arise," says the Lord."*
>
> For the Lord himself in the gospel pitied his people this way, because they had no ruler, when they could well obey. Thus it is also said in the gospel, "The harvest is plenteous, but the laborers are few."
>
> But we must understand this as spoken in the person of God the Father, who, because of the needy and the poor—that is, the people who in need and poverty were lacking spiritual good things, was good enough to send his own Son. Thus begins his Sermon on the Mount in Matthew, where he says, "Blessed are the poor in spirit: for theirs is the kingdom of heaven."
>
> "I will place him in the safety for which he longs."

He does not say whom he would place, but "in safety" must be understood as "in Christ," as in the verse, "For my eyes have seen your salvation." This means that he placed in him what he needs in order to take away the wretchedness of the needy, and comforting the sighing of the poor. . . .

"The promises of the Lord are promises that are pure."

This is spoken in the person of the prophet himself, "The promises of the Lord are promises that are pure." He says "pure," meaning without the alloy of pretense. For many preach the truth impurely: they sell it for the bribe of the advantages of this life. About such people the Apostle says that they did not declare Christ purely.

"Silver refined in a furnace on the ground."

These words of the Lord refer to the tribulations approved to sinners.

"Purified seven times:" by the fear of God, by godliness, by knowledge, by might, by counsel, by understanding, by wisdom.

For there are also seven steps of beatitude, which the Lord goes over, according to Matthew, in the same Sermon on the Mount:

> Blessed are the poor in spirit,
> blessed are the meek,
> blessed are they that mourn,
> blessed are they who hunger and thirst after
>   righteousness,
> blessed are the merciful,
> blessed are the pure in heart,
> blessed are the peacemakers.

You may notice how all that long sermon was based on these seven sentences. For the eighth where it is said, "Blessed are they who suffer persecution for righteousness' sake," denotes the fire itself, by which the silver is purified seven times.

—St. Augustine, Expositions on the Psalms

> **Questions to Think About**
> 1. How often do I let the wickedness of the world infect me with despair? What could I do to overcome such feelings?
> 2. When I've felt persecuted or put upon, how do I respond? Have I remembered to be grateful for my purification?

Psalm 15

This very practical psalm outlines just what it means to live a life pleasing to God. The truly faithful will not speak unkindly or take advantage of their neighbors, but will always try to do what they know is right.

A Psalm of David.

O Lord, who shall sojourn in your tent?
    Who shall dwell on your holy hill?

He who walks blamelessly, and does what is right,
    and speaks truth from his heart;
who does not slander with his tongue,
    and does no evil to his friend,
    nor takes up a reproach against his neighbor;
in whose eyes a reprobate is despised,
    but who honors those who fear the Lord;
who swears to his own hurt and does not change;
who does not put out his money at interest,
    and does not take a bribe against the innocent.

He who does these things shall never be moved.

> **Words to Remember**
> Who shall dwell on your holy hill?
> He who walks blamelessly, and does what is right.

Rich Brevity

In one of his last general audiences, Pope John Paul II quoted this selection from St. Hilary of Poitiers to show us that this short psalm points our way home to heaven. The pope noted that St. Hilary links the psalm's finale to the initial image of the tent of the Temple of Zion:

> Acting in accordance with these precepts, we dwell in the tent and rest on the mountain. May the preservation of the precepts and the work of the commandments, therefore, endure unchanged. This psalm must be anchored in our inmost depths, it must be engraved on our hearts, stored in our memories; the treasure of its rich brevity must confront us night and day. Thus, having acquired its riches on our way toward eternity and dwelling in the Church, we will be able to rest at last in the glory of Christ's Body.

—St. Hilary of Poitiers, *Homilies on the Psalms*

Questions to Think About
1. Do I fully appreciate that the presence of God is no longer confined to a tent or even a temple, but "the dwelling of God is with men" (Revelation 21:3)?
2. How does the Church function like the ancient Tent of the Divine Presence?

Psalm 19

The glory of creation is celebrated in this psalm. When we look at the magnificence of the universe, we see the glory of God revealed. The beauty of creation itself should be a constant reminder to us to live a life pleasing to the Creator.

To the choirmaster.
A Psalm of David.

The heavens are telling the glory of God;
    and the firmament proclaims his handiwork.
Day to day pours forth speech,
    and night to night declares knowledge.
There is no speech, nor are there words;
    their voice is not heard;
yet their voice goes out through all the earth,
    and their words to the end of the world.

In them he has set a tent for the sun,
which comes forth like a bridegroom leaving his chamber,
    and like a strong man runs its course with joy.
Its rising is from the end of the heavens,
    and its circuit to the end of them;
    and there is nothing hid from its heat.

The law of the LORD is perfect,
    reviving the soul;
the testimony of the LORD is sure,

making wise the simple;
the precepts of the LORD are right,
   rejoicing the heart;
the commandment of the LORD is pure,
   enlightening the eyes;
the fear of the LORD is clean,
   enduring for ever;
the ordinances of the LORD are true,
   and righteous altogether.
More to be desired are they than gold,
   even much fine gold;
sweeter also than honey
   and drippings of the honeycomb.

Moreover by them is thy servant warned;
   in keeping them there is great reward.
But who can discern his errors?
   Clear me from hidden faults.
Keep back your servant also from presumptuous sins;
   let them not have dominion over me!
Then I shall be blameless,
   and innocent of great transgression.

Let the words of my mouth and the meditation of my heart
   be acceptable in thy sight,
   O LORD, my rock and my redeemer.

Words to Remember
The heavens are telling the glory of God;
   and the firmament proclaims his handiwork.

All Creation Shows Us the Truth about God

In explaining what St. Paul meant when he said that God's nature has been clearly perceived in creation, St. John Chrysostom comes back to Psalm 19. Everything in creation shows the power and wisdom of God, and the beauty and wonder of the world is meant to draw us closer to him.

> "Ever since the creation of the world his invisible nature, namely, his eternal power and deity, has been clearly perceived in the things that have been made" (Romans 1:20).
>
> In the same way, the prophet said, "The heavens are telling the glory of God" (Psalm 19:1).
>
> For what will the pagans say in that day? "We didn't know about you"? Didn't you hear the heaven sending forth a voice by the sight, while the well-ordered harmony of all things spoke out more clearly than a trumpet? Didn't you see the hours of night and day abiding unmoved continually, the goodly order of winter, spring, and the other seasons remaining sure and unmoved, the regularity of the sea amid all its turbulence and waves? All things abiding in order—and by their beauty and their grandeur, loudly preaching the Creator!
>
> For all these things, and more than these, Paul sums up in saying, "The invisible things of him from the creation of the world are clearly seen, being understood by the things which are made, even his eternal Power and Godhead; so that they are without excuse."
>
> And yet this is not the reason why God has made these things, even if this is what came of it. For it was not to leave them without any excuse that he set before

them so great a system of teaching, but so that they might come to know him. But by not having recognized him, they deprived themselves of every excuse. And then to show how they are bereft of excuse, he says, "for although they knew God they did not honor him as God or give thanks to him" (Romans 19:21).

—St. John Chrysostom, *Homilies on Romans*

Questions to Think About
1. How could I grow in appreciation of the beauty in the humblest things around me?
2. Do I regularly thank God for the goodness of creation?

Psalm 22

Every Christian since Christ himself has seen in this psalm a graphically accurate description of the crucifixion. "My God, My God, why have you forsaken me?" was Jesus' loud cry on the cross. Yet it was not a cry of despair, for the psalm ends in triumph: the faithful to come will proclaim the Lord's deliverance "to a people yet unborn."

To the choirmaster: according to The Hind of the Dawn. A Psalm of David.

My God, my God, why have you forsaken me?
   Why are you so far from helping me, from the
      words of my groaning?
O my God, I cry by day, but you do not answer;
   and by night, but find no rest.

Yet you are holy,
   enthroned on the praises of Israel.
In you our fathers trusted;
   they trusted, and you delivered them.
To you they cried, and were saved;
   in you they trusted, and were not disappointed.

But I am a worm, and no man;
   scorned by men, and despised by the people.
All who see me mock at me,
   they make mouths at me, they wag their heads;

"He committed his cause to the LORD; let him deliver him,
   let him rescue him, for he delights in him!"

Yet you are he who took me from the womb;
   you kept me safe upon my mother's breasts.
Upon you was I cast from my birth,
   and since my mother bore me you have been my God.
Be not far from me,
   for trouble is near
   and there is none to help.

Many bulls encompass me,
   strong bulls of Bashan surround me;
they open wide their mouths at me,
   like a ravening and roaring lion.

I am poured out like water,
   and all my bones are out of joint;
my heart is like wax,
   it is melted within my breast;
my strength is dried up like a potsherd,
   and my tongue cleaves to my jaws;
   thou dost lay me in the dust of death.

Yes, dogs are round about me;
   a company of evildoers encircle me;
   they have pierced my hands and feet—
I can count all my bones—
   they stare and gloat over me;
they divide my garments among them,
   and for my clothing they cast lots.

But you, O Lord, be not far off!
  O my help, hasten to my aid!
Deliver my soul from the sword,
  my life from the power of the dog!
Save me from the mouth of the lion,
  my afflicted soul from the horns of the wild oxen!

I will tell of your name to my brethren;
  in the midst of the congregation I will praise you:
You who fear the Lord, praise him!
  all you sons of Jacob, glorify him,
  and stand in awe of him, all you sons of Israel!
For he has not despised or abhorred
  the affliction of the afflicted;
and he has not hidden his face from him,
  but has heard, when he cried to him.

From you comes my praise in the great congregation;
  my vows I will pay before those who fear him.
The afflicted shall eat and be satisfied;
  those who seek him shall praise the Lord!
  May your hearts live for ever!

All the ends of the earth shall remember
  and turn to the Lord;
and all the families of the nations
  shall worship before him.
For dominion belongs to the Lord,
  and he rules over the nations.

Yes, to him shall all the proud of the earth bow down;
  before him shall bow all who go down to the dust,
  and he who cannot keep himself alive.

Posterity shall serve him;
>   men shall tell of the Lord to the coming generation,
and proclaim his deliverance to a people yet unborn,
>   that he has wrought it.

> **Words to Remember**
> Yet you are he who took me from the womb;
>   you kept me safe upon my mother's breasts.
> Upon you was I cast from my birth,
>   and since my mother bore me you have been my God.

"None to Help"

What could it mean for God to have "forsaken" the Son? Eusebius answers that Christ chose to refer to this psalm on the cross to point out that the victory over death was his alone.

> *"Trouble is near, and there is none to help"?*
>
> Of course no one could expect that any of the evil enemy powers would work with Christ or help him in his mission of good. But surely what was bitterest in his cup of pain was this: that none of the good angels, and none of the divine powers, dared to venture to the halls of Death and help him in rescuing the souls there....
>
> So naturally he cries out, "Trouble is near, and there is none to help!" The only Being from heaven who could have helped him had forsaken him, so that everyone would know the glory and independence of his own choice and of his own victory. And since the only Being that could help him was not then his

helper, it is natural that his first words should be, "Eli, Eli, lama sabachthani?"—that is, "My God, My God, why hast thou forsaken me?"

His Father's power was with him when he was conceived, and when the Holy Virgin bore him—when the Holy Spirit came upon the maiden, and the Power of the Most High overshadowed her, and the Father himself drew forth the Son from her womb. But when in the hour of his Passion he began his struggle with Death, the helper was no longer with him.

This is what he himself tells us, and I believe it. What else could those words mean that he spoke on the Cross? "Eli, Eli, lama sabachthani"—words that were prophetically foretold in the psalm. Like a great athlete, he took on all these adversaries, while Almighty God supervised the contest and gave the decision.

So he summons his Father as the overseer of what is being done, and as the adviser, like a clever Anointer, to come to him—especially since he has no other helper, but only the One who governs the contest. And so he says in prayer, "Be not far from me, for trouble is near, and there is none to help."

—Eusebius, *Demonstration of the Gospel*

Questions to Think About
1. Do my current trials or struggles blind me to the gift of God's salvation? How can I see beyond my troubles to the glory that awaits me?
2. Am I able to praise God even when "I am poured out like water"? Why or why not?

Psalm 23

Without a doubt, this is the most popular of all the psalms. And it deserves its reputation: it's one of the greatest poems of all time. Like a great painting, it balances light and darkness in perfect proportion so that the darkness emphasizes the light.

A Psalm of David.

The LORD is my shepherd, I shall not want;
    he makes me lie down in green pastures.
He leads me beside still waters;
    he restores my soul.
He leads me in paths of righteousness
    for his name's sake.

Even though I walk through the valley of the shadow
    of death,
    I fear no evil;
for you are with me;
    your rod and your staff,
    they comfort me.

You prepare a table before me
    in the presence of my enemies;
you anoint my head with oil,
    my cup overflows.
Surely goodness and mercy shall follow me
    all the days of my life;

and I shall dwell in the house of the LORD
   for ever.

> **Words to Remember**
> Even though I walk through the valley of the shadow
>   of death,
>   I fear no evil;
> for you are with me.

The Lord's Table

For a Christian, the "table" that God prepares before us suggests the table of the Eucharist, in which God himself provides the meal.

> Blessed David tells the meaning of this, saying, *"You prepare a table before me in the presence of my enemies."* This is what he means: Before you came, the evil spirits prepared a table for men, polluted and defiled and full of devilish influence; but since your coming, O Lord, you have prepared a table before me.
>
> When the man says to God, "you prepare a table before me," what can he mean? It must be that mystical and spiritual Table which God has prepared for us—in the presence of our enemies, meaning in opposition to the evil spirits. And he speaks very truly. For the old table had communion with devils, but this new table has communion with God.
>
> *"You anoint my head with oil."* He anointed your forehead with oil, which is your seal from God, so that

you may become the engraving of the signet, "Holiness unto God."

"*My cup overflows.*" This is the cup that Jesus took in his hands, and gave thanks, and said, "This is My blood, which is shed for many for the remission of sins" (Matthew 26:28).

—St. Cyril of Jerusalem, *Catechetical Lectures*

The same St. Cyril reminds us that we have another source of spiritual nourishment: the Word of God, as revealed in Scripture.

> Nourish your soul with sacred readings; for the Lord has prepared a spiritual table for you. So you should say, just like the psalmist, "The LORD is my shepherd, I shall not want; he makes me lie down in green pastures; he leads me beside still waters; he restores my soul."
>
> Say it so that angels may also share your joy, and Christ himself, the great High Priest, having accepted your resolve, may present you all to the Father, saying, "Behold, I and the children whom God has given me" (Isaiah 8:18).
>
> May he keep you all well-pleasing in his sight! To him be the glory, and the power to the endless ages of eternity. Amen.

—St. Cyril of Jerusalem, *Catechetical Lectures*

Questions to Think About
1. In the darkest times, do I turn to the Eucharist—the table God prepares before me?
2. How can a constant awareness of my baptism, when I was marked with the sign of the cross forever, help me in my spiritual journey?

Psalm 27

In some ways this psalm is like an extended version of Psalm 23. The theme is similar: though darkness and enemies may surround us, God keeps us safe and never lets us out of his care.

A Psalm of David.

The Lord is my light and my salvation;
    whom shall I fear?
The Lord is the stronghold of my life;
    of whom shall I be afraid?

When evildoers assail me,
    uttering slanders against me,
my adversaries and foes,
    they shall stumble and fall.

Though a host encamp against me,
    my heart shall not fear;
though war arise against me,
    yet I will be confident.

One thing have I asked of the Lord,
    that will I seek after;
that I may dwell in the house of the Lord
    all the days of my life,
to behold the beauty of the Lord,
    and to inquire in his temple.

For he will hide me in his shelter
   in the day of trouble;
he will conceal me under the cover of his tent,
   he will set me high upon a rock.

And now my head shall be lifted up
   above my enemies round about me;
and I will offer in his tent
   sacrifices with shouts of joy;
I will sing and make melody to the LORD.

Hear, O LORD, when I cry aloud,
   be gracious to me and answer me!
You have said, "Seek my face."
   My heart says to you,
"Your face, LORD, do I seek."
   Hide not your face from me.

Turn not your servant away in anger,
   you who have been my help.
Cast me not off, forsake me not,
   O God of my salvation!
For my father and my mother have forsaken me,
   but the LORD will take me up.

Teach me your way, O LORD;
   and lead me on a level path
   because of my enemies.
Give me not up to the will of my adversaries;
   for false witnesses have risen against me,
   and they breathe out violence.

I believe that I shall see the goodness of the Lord
   in the land of the living!
Wait for the Lord;
   be strong, and let your heart take courage;
   yea, wait for the Lord!

> **Words to Remember**
> I believe that I shall see the goodness of the Lord
>   in the land of the living!

Wrestling with Angels

Who are our adversaries? Certainly we have plenty of human enemies, but Origen reminds us that our greatest foes are spiritual beings that are far more powerful than we are. We could never overcome them without help. Fortunately, we have help, and we must keep up our faith.

> I do not think that human nature by itself can keep up a struggle with angels, and with the powers of the height and of the abyss, and with any other creature; but when it feels the presence of the Lord dwelling within it, confidence in the divine help will lead it to say, "The Lord is my light, and my salvation; whom shall I fear? The Lord is the protector of my life; of whom shall I be afraid? When the enemies draw near to me, to eat my flesh, my enemies who trouble me, they stumbled and fell. Though an host encamp against me, my heart shall not fear; though war should rise against me, in Him shall I be confident."

All this leads me to believe that a man might never be able to vanquish an opposing power by himself, unless he had the benefit of divine assistance.

—Origen, *On First Principles*

Spiritual Combat

Satan, the ancient serpent, holds the power to harass us with physical suffering, but the decline of our bodies can serve to refine our soul. St. Ambrose shows us that this is the message of Jesus, confirmed by the lives of the saints.

> Do not fear if your flesh is eaten away; the soul is not consumed. And so David says that he does not fear, because the enemy is eating up his flesh but not his soul, as we read: "When evildoers assail me, uttering slanders against me, my adversaries and foes, they shall stumble and fall." So the serpent's work is his own downfall . . . and the overthrow of the serpent may be the raising again of the man who had been cast down. Scripture testifies that Satan is the author of this bodily suffering and weakness of the flesh, where Paul says: "And to keep me from being too elated by the abundance of revelations, a thorn was given me in the flesh, a messenger of Satan, to harass me, to keep me from being too elated" (2 Corinthians 12:7). So Paul learned to heal even as he himself had been made whole.

—St. Ambrose of Milan, *On Repentance*

Questions to Think About
1. How often do I "sing and make melody to the Lord"? Is it a constant habit? Do I do it even when I'm surrounded by troubles?
2. How might I grow in faith so that I can trust in God at all times, even when I can't see his protection working at the moment?

Psalm 29

This is a hymn to God's glory. Praise is the theme and the only subject. In a series of vivid images, the psalmist tries to express how much the glory of God exceeds the most glorious things we can imagine.

A Psalm of David.

Ascribe to the Lord, O heavenly beings,
    ascribe to the Lord glory and strength.
Ascribe to the Lord the glory of his name;
    worship the Lord in holy array.

The voice of the Lord is upon the waters;
    the God of glory thunders,
    the Lord, upon many waters.
The voice of the Lord is powerful,
    the voice of the Lord is full of majesty.

The voice of the Lord breaks the cedars,
    the Lord breaks the cedars of Lebanon.
He makes Lebanon to skip like a calf,
    and Sirion like a young wild ox.

The voice of the Lord flashes forth flames of fire.
The voice of the Lord shakes the wilderness,
    the Lord shakes the wilderness of Kadesh.

The voice of the LORD makes the oaks to whirl,
   and strips the forests bare;
   and in his temple all cry, "Glory!"

The LORD sits enthroned over the flood;
   the LORD sits enthroned as king for ever.
May the LORD give strength to his people!
   May the LORD bless his people with peace!

> **Words to Remember**
> The voice of the LORD is upon the waters;
>   the God of glory thunders,
>   the LORD, upon many waters.

The Voice of the Lord

St. Gregory of Nyssa relates the images in this psalm to the heavenly voice heard at the baptism of Christ.

> The inspired David foretold the voice of the Father from heaven when the Son was baptized. At that time the Father spoke so that he might lead the hearers, who till then had seen only the lowly human who was perceptible by their senses, to see the dignity of nature that belongs to the Godhead. And so David wrote in his book that passage, "The voice of the Lord is upon the waters; the God of glory thunders, the Lord, upon many waters."
>
>   —St. Gregory of Nyssa, *On the Baptism of Christ*

St. Augustine interprets one of the images as a metaphor for the spread of the knowledge of God to the Gentiles. The "wilderness" is the world where God's word is unknown.

> "*The voice of the* LORD *shakes the wilderness.*" The voice of the Lord moves the Gentiles toward the faith—the Gentiles who were once without hope, and without God in the world (Ephesians 2:12), where no prophet, no preacher of God's word, as it were, no man had dwelt. "*The* LORD *shakes the wilderness of Kadesh.*" And then the Lord will cause the holy word of his Scriptures to be fully known
>
> —St. Augustine, *Expositions on the Psalms*

Questions to Think About
1. Is simple praise to God a regular part of my prayer time? A regular part of my day?
2. Can I hear God's voice when it is "thundering"—in Scripture, from the pulpit, or in the glories of creation? How can I grow more sensitive to the Lord's voice?

Psalm 32

Sin brings sorrow, and sorrow can lead to repentance or despair. Despair gets us nowhere, but repentance brings joy: the joy of knowing God's forgiveness, and a restored relationship with the Lord.

> *A Psalm of David.*
> *A Maskil.*

Blessed is he whose transgression is forgiven,
    whose sin is covered.
Blessed is the man to whom the L<small>ORD</small> imputes no
    iniquity,
    and in whose spirit there is no deceit.

When I declared not my sin, my body wasted away
    through my groaning all day long.
For day and night thy hand was heavy upon me;
    my strength was dried up as by the heat of summer.
      Selah

I acknowledged my sin to you,
    and I did not hide my iniquity;
I said, "I will confess my transgressions to the L<small>ORD</small>";
    then you forgave the guilt of my sin. *Selah*

Therefore let every one who is godly
    offer prayer to you;

at a time of distress, in the rush of great waters,
>   they shall not reach him.
You are a hiding place for me,
>   you preserve me from trouble;
>   you surround me with deliverance. *Selah*

I will instruct you and teach you
>   the way you should go;
>   I will counsel you with my eye upon you.
Be not like a horse or a mule, without understanding,
>   which must be curbed with bit and bridle,
>   else it will not keep with you.

Many are the pangs of the wicked;
>   but steadfast love surrounds him who trusts in the Lord.
Be glad in the Lord, and rejoice, O righteous,
>   and shout for joy, all you upright in heart!

Words to Remember

I acknowledged my sin to you,
>   and I did not hide my iniquity;
I said, "I will confess my transgressions to the Lord";
>   then you forgave the guilt of my sin.

"Let Us Purify Ourselves by Tears"

St. Ambrose tells us that God really does value our tears of repentance. Referring to the words of the Lord about Ephraim in Jeremiah 31, Ambrose assures us that the sinner who turns from the sin can take comfort in the promise of the sacraments.

☙ But the apostles—whom Christ had taught to baptize—taught repentance, promised forgiveness, and remitted guilt. This is what David taught when he said, "Blessed is he whose transgression is forgiven, whose sin is covered. Blessed is the man to whom the Lord imputes no iniquity." He calls them both blessed: both the one whose sins are remitted by the font, and the one whose sin is covered by good works. For he who repents ought not only to wash away his sin by his tears, but also to cover and hide his former transgressions by doing better, so that sin may not be imputed to him.

Then let us cover our falls by our subsequent acts; let us purify ourselves by tears, so that the Lord our God may hear us when we lament, as he heard Ephraim weeping, as it is written: "I have surely heard Ephraim weeping." And he expressly repeats the very words of Ephraim: "You have chastised me and I was chastised, like a calf I was not trained."

For a calf plays and leaves its stall, and so Ephraim was untrained like a calf far away from the stall; because he had forsaken the stall of the Lord, followed Jeroboam (Sirach 47:23), and worshiped the calves—a future event that was prophetically indicated through Aaron in Exodus 31, which foretold that the people of the Jews would fall after this manner.

And so repenting, Ephraim says: "Turn me, and I shall be turned, for you are the Lord my God. Surely in the end of my captivity I repented, and after I learned I mourned over the days of confusion, and subjected myself to you because I received reproach and made you known."

We see how to repent—the words we should say and the things we should do. The time of sin is called "a time of distress," for there is distress when Christ is denied.

Let us, then, submit ourselves to God, and not be subject to sin. And when we remember our sins, let us blush as though at some disgrace, and not boast about them the way some boast of overcoming modesty or putting down the feeling of justice. Let our conversion be such, that we who did not know God may now ourselves declare him to others, so that the Lord, moved by such a conversion on our part, may answer to us: "Ephraim is from youth a dear son, a pleasant child, for since my words are concerning him, I will truly remember him, therefore have I hastened to be over him; I will surely have mercy on him, says the Lord."

And the Lord also shows what mercy he promises us when he says further on: "I have satiated every thirsty soul, and have satisfied every hungry soul. Therefore, I awaked and beheld, and my sleep was sweet unto me." We observe that the Lord promises his sacraments to those who sin. Let us, then, all be converted to the Lord.

—St. Ambrose, *On Repentance*

Questions to Think About
1. Do I regularly confess the sins that prey on my conscience?
2. What obstacles keep me from making frequent use of the sacrament God offers to repentant sinners?

Psalm 34

The superscription puts this psalm in context: it was composed at a time when David had to use all his cleverness and even deviousness just to stay alive. Yet David knew that, ultimately, it was never his own strategy that saved him, and in these difficult circumstances he sings one of the most memorable hymns of praise to God in the whole Bible.

> *A Psalm of David,*
> *when he feigned madness before Abimelech, so that he*
> *drove him out, and he went away.*

> I will bless the Lord at all times;
>   his praise shall continually be in my mouth.
> My soul makes its boast in the Lord;
>   let the afflicted hear and be glad.
> O magnify the Lord with me,
>   and let us exalt his name together!
>
> I sought the Lord, and he answered me,
>   and delivered me from all my fears.
> Look to him, and be radiant;
>   so your faces shall never be ashamed.
> This poor man cried, and the Lord heard him,
>   and saved him out of all his troubles.
> The angel of the Lord encamps
>   around those who fear him, and delivers them.
> O taste and see that the Lord is good!
>   Blessed is the man who takes refuge in him!

O fear the Lord, you his saints,
  for those who fear him have no want!
The young lions suffer want and hunger;
  but those who seek the Lord lack no good thing.

Come, O sons, listen to me,
  I will teach you the fear of the Lord.
What man is there who desires life,
  and covets many days, that he may enjoy good?
Keep your tongue from evil,
  and your lips from speaking deceit.
Depart from evil, and do good;
  seek peace, and pursue it.

The eyes of the Lord are toward the righteous,
  and his ears toward their cry.
The face of the Lord is against evildoers,
  to cut off the remembrance of them from the earth.
When the righteous cry for help, the Lord hears,
  and delivers them out of all their troubles.
The Lord is near to the brokenhearted,
  and saves the crushed in spirit.

Many are the afflictions of the righteous;
  but the Lord delivers him out of them all.
He keeps all his bones;
  not one of them is broken.
Evil shall slay the wicked;
  and those who hate the righteous will be
    condemned.
The Lord redeems the life of his servants;
  none of those who take refuge in him will be
    condemned.

> **Words to Remember**
> O taste and see that the Lord is good!
> Happy is the man who takes refuge in him!

Taste and See

The famous words "O taste and see that the Lord is good" inevitably led early Christians to meditate on the Eucharist. Here three great Christian writers examine what it means to "taste and see."

> After this you hear the chanter inviting you with a sacred melody to the communion of the Holy Mysteries, and saying, "O taste and see that the Lord is good." Do not leave the judgment to your bodily taste, no, but to unfaltering faith; for they who taste are bidden to taste, not bread and wine, but the long-prophesied Body and Blood of Christ.
>
> So when you approach, do no come with your wrists extended, or your fingers spread; but make your left hand a throne for the right, for your right hand is to receive a King. And having hollowed your palm, receive the Body of Christ, saying over it, "Amen." So then, after having carefully hallowed your eyes by the touch of the holy Body, partake of it. Make sure you do not lose any of it; for whatever you lose is obviously as much a loss as if you lost an arm or a leg.
>
> For tell me, if any one gave you grains of gold, would you not hold them with all carefulness, making sure you did not lose a single one of them? Then will you not be all the more careful to make sure that not

a crumb falls from you of what is more precious than gold and precious stones?

Then after you have partaken of the Body of Christ, draw near also to the cup of his Blood. Do not stretch out your hands, but bend, and saying with an air of worship and reverence, "Amen," hallow yourself by partaking also of the Blood of Christ. And while the moisture is still upon your lips, touch it with your hands, and hallow your eyes and brow and the other organs of sense. Then wait for the prayer, and give thanks to God, who has accounted you worthy of such great mysteries.

Hold fast these traditions undefiled, and keep yourselves free from offense. Do not separate yourselves from the Communion; do not deprive yourselves, through the pollution of sins, of these holy and spiritual mysteries. And may the God of peace sanctify you wholly; and may your spirit, and soul, and body be preserved whole without blame at the coming of our Lord Jesus Christ. To whom be glory and honor and might, with the Father and the Holy Spirit, now and ever, and world without end. Amen.

—St. Cyril of Jerusalem, *Catechetical Lectures*

"O taste and see that the Lord is good!" You will not taste, and you say, "Is it pleasant?" What does "pleasant" mean? If you have tasted, let us see it in your fruit, not just in your words, as if you bore only leaves, lest you should deserve to wither as the fig-tree was withered by the curse of God (Matthew 21:19).

"Taste," he says, "and see that the Lord is good." Taste and see: you shall see if you have tasted. But how do you prove it to someone who does not taste? Whatever you say in praise of the pleasantness of the name of God is mere words: taste is another thing. Even the ungodly hear the words of his praise, but only the saints taste how sweet it is.

And what does a man do who knows how sweet the name of God is, and wishes to reveal and show it to someone, and finds no one to whom he can reveal it? For there is no need to reveal it to the saints, because they themselves taste it and know, but the ungodly cannot know what they will not taste ... I know how sweet it is, but only to those who have tasted.

—St. Augustine, *Expositions on the Psalms*

I am covetous of God's bounty; and as he is never slack in giving, so I am never weary in receiving. The more I drink, the more I thirst. For I have read the song of the psalmist: "O taste and see that the Lord is good." Every good thing that we have is a tasting of the Lord. When I fancy myself to have finished the book of virtue, I shall then only be at the beginning.

—St. Jerome, *Letters*

> **Questions to Think About**
> 1. How can I better approach the Eucharist with a real sense of the value of the gift I'm about to receive?
> 2. What are all the things that I enjoy most? How can I thank God for them?

Psalm 40

David's songs of pleading and lamentation are turned to a "new song": "a song of praise to our God." Here David makes the surprising declaration that God doesn't want sacrifices and burnt offerings—what he really desires is that we should take delight in doing his will. Although God has delivered him for the time being, David is still in a dangerous situation and prays that the deliverance will continue—but he prays with confidence, knowing that God will keep his promises.

To the choirmaster.
A Psalm of David.

I waited patiently for the Lord;
   he inclined to me and heard my cry.
He drew me up from the desolate pit,
   out of the miry bog,
and set my feet upon a rock,
   making my steps secure.
He put a new song in my mouth,
   a song of praise to our God.
Many will see and fear,
   and put their trust in the Lord.

Blessed is the man who makes
   the Lord his trust,
who does not turn to the proud,
   to those who go astray after false gods!

You have multiplied, O Lord my God,
   your wondrous deeds and your thoughts toward us;
   none can compare with thee!
Were I to proclaim and tell of them,
   they would be more than can be numbered.

Sacrifice and offering you do not desire;
   but you have given me an open ear.
Burnt offering and sin offering
   You have not required.
Then I said, "Behold, I come;
   in the roll of the book it is written of me;
I delight to do your will, O my God;
   your law is within my heart."

I have told the glad news of deliverance
   in the great congregation;
behold, I have not restrained my lips,
   as you know, O Lord.
I have not hidden your saving help within my heart,
   I have spoken of your faithfulness and your
     salvation;
I have not concealed your mercy and your
     faithfulness
   from the great congregation.

Do not thou, O Lord, withhold
   Your compassion from me,
let your mercy and your faithfulness
   ever preserve me!
For evils have encompassed me
   without number;

my iniquities have overtaken me,
>   till I cannot see;
they are more than the hairs of my head;
>   my heart fails me.

Be pleased, O Lord, to deliver me!
>   O Lord, make haste to help me!
Let them be put to shame and confusion altogether
>   who seek to snatch away my life;
let them be turned back and brought to dishonor
>   who desire my hurt!
Let them be appalled because of their shame
>   who say to me, "Aha, Aha!"

But may all who seek you
>   rejoice and be glad in you;
may those who love your salvation
>   say continually, "Great is the Lord!"
As for me, I am poor and needy;
>   but the Lord takes thought for me.
You are my help and my deliverer;
>   do not tarry, O my God!

Words to Remember

I have not hidden your saving help within my heart,
>   I have spoken of your faithfulness and your
>>   salvation;
I have not concealed your mercy and thy faithfulness
>   from the great congregation.

The New Song

What does it mean to say that God does not desire sacrifice and offering? Eusebius explains this as the "new song" that the Lord puts in the mouth of the psalmist. God no longer desires sacrifice because God himself has provided the perfect sacrifice in Jesus Christ, which is present to us every time we celebrate the Eucharist.

> The wondrous David, inspired by the Holy Spirit to foresee the future, foretold in these words:
>
>> He drew me up from the desolate pit,
>>   out of the miry bog,
>> and set my feet upon a rock,
>>   making my steps secure.
>> He put a new song in my mouth,
>>   a song of praise to our God.
>
> And he shows clearly what the "new song" is when he goes on to say:
>
>> Sacrifice and offering thou dost not desire;
>>   but thou hast given me an open ear.
>> Burnt offering and sin offering
>>   thou hast not required.
>> Then I said, "Lo, I come;
>>   in the roll of the book it is written of me;
>> I delight to do thy will, O my God;
>>   thy law is within my heart."
>
> And he adds: "I have told the glad news of deliverance in the great congregation." He plainly teaches

that, in place of the ancient sacrifices and whole burnt-offerings, the incarnate presence of Christ that was prepared was offered. And this very thing he proclaims to his Church as a great mystery expressed with prophetic voice in the book.

As we have been given a memorial of this offering, which we celebrate on a table by means of signs of his Body and saving Blood according to the laws of the new covenant, we are taught again by the prophet David to say:

> Thou preparest a table before me
> >in the presence of my enemies;
> thou anointest my head with oil,
> >my cup overflows. (Psalm 23:5)

Here it is plainly the mystic chrism and the holy sacrifices of Christ's table that are meant, by which we are taught to offer to almighty God through our great High Priest all through our life the celebration of our sacrifices, bloodless, reasonable, and well-pleasing to him.

—Eusebius, *Demonstration of the Gospel*

Questions to Think About

1. Why was David able to trust in God's promises? How can I grow in confidence so as to trust the way David did?
2. Have often do I hide God's saving help within my heart? How can I better communicate the glad news of deliverance?

Psalm 42

This has all the elements of a love song—the unbearable longing, the near despair when the beloved appears to be far away, and the loving memory of the beloved's attributes. But the beloved is God. The psalmist uses what were even then romantic conventions as the only language strong enough to express the depth of his love for the Lord.

> *To the choirmaster.*
> *A Maskil of the Sons of Korah.*

As a deer longs
    for flowing streams,
so longs my soul
    for you, O God.
My soul thirsts for God,
    for the living God.
When shall I come and behold
    the face of God?
My tears have been my food
    day and night,
while men say to me continually,
    "Where is your God?"

These things I remember,
    as I pour out my soul:
how I went with the throng,
    and led them in procession to the house of God,

with glad shouts and songs of thanksgiving,
    a multitude keeping festival.
Why are you cast down, O my soul,
    and why are you disquieted within me?
Hope in God; for I shall again praise him,
    my savior and my God.

My soul is cast down within me,
    therefore I remember you
from the land of Jordan and of Hermon,
    from Mount Mizar.
Deep calls to deep
    at the thunder of your cataracts;
all your waves and your billows
    have gone over me.
By day the Lord commands his steadfast love;
    and at night his song is with me,
    a prayer to the God of my life.

I say to God, my rock:
    "Why hast thou forgotten me?
Why do I go mourning
    because of the oppression of the enemy?"
As with a deadly wound in my body,
    my adversaries taunt me,
while they say to me continually,
    "Where is your God?"

Why are you cast down, O my soul,
    and why are you disquieted within me?
Hope in God; for I shall again praise him,
    my help and my God.

> **Words to Remember**
> Why are you cast down, O my soul,
>   and why are you disquieted within me?
> Hope in God; for I shall again praise him,
>   my help and my God.

Run to the Brooks

If we can turn our longing away from vice and self-indulgence and toward the word of God, says St. Augustine, we can know the same love the psalmist expressed in this psalm.

> We have undertaken the exposition of a psalm corresponding to your own longings, on which we propose to speak to you. For the psalm itself begins with a certain pious longing; and he who sings it says, "As a hart longs for flowing streams, so longs my soul for thee, O God."
>
> Who is it then that says this? It is ourselves, if we be but willing! And why ask who it is other than yourself, when you can be the thing you are asking about?
>
> It is not however one individual, but it is one Body; but Christ's Body is the Church (Colossians 1:24). Such longing indeed is not found in all who enter the Church; but if you have tasted the sweetness of the Lord, and own in Christ that for which you long, do not think that you are the only ones, but know that there are such seeds scattered throughout the field of the Lord, this whole earth. Know that there is a certain Christian unity, whose voice says, "As a hart longs for flowing streams, so longs my soul for thee, O God."

And indeed we could understand it as the cry of those who, being as yet catechumens, are hastening to the grace of the holy Font. For that reason this psalm is ordinarily chanted on those occasions, so that they may long for the fountain of remission of sins, even as the hart for the flowing streams. Let this be allowed; and this meaning retain its place in the Church; a place both truthful and sanctioned by usage.

Nevertheless, it appears to me, my brethren, that such a longing is not fully satisfied even in the faithful in baptism; but that perhaps, if they know where they are right now, and where they have to go from here, their longing blazes up even brighter. . . .

Let then our understanding be roused: and if the psalm be sung to us, let us follow it with our understanding. . . . Run to the flowing streams; long after the flowing streams.

"With God is the fountain of Life"; a fountain that shall never be dried up: in his Light is a Light that shall never be darkened. Long for this light: for a certain fountain, a certain light, such as your bodily eyes know not; a light to see which the inward eye must be prepared; a fountain, to drink of which the inward thirst is to be kindled.

Run to the fountain; long for the fountain. . . . . Do not be satisfied with running like any ordinary animal; run like the hart. What do we mean by "like the hart"? Let there be no sloth in your running; run with all your might: long for the fountain with all your might. For we find in the hart an emblem of swiftness.

But perhaps Scripture meant us to consider in the stag not this point only, but another as well.

Hear what else there is in the hart. It destroys serpents, and after killing serpents, it is inflamed with thirst yet more violent; having destroyed serpents, it runs to the "flowing streams," with a keener thirst than before.

The serpents are your vices. Destroy the serpents of iniquity; then will you long yet more for "the Fountain of Truth." Perhaps avarice whispers in your ear some dark counsel, hisses against the word of God, hisses against the commandment of God. And if you hear "Disregard this or that, if you prefer working iniquity to despising some temporal good," you choose to be bitten by a serpent, rather than destroy it.

While you are still indulgent to your vice, your covetousness, or your appetite, when am I to find in you a "longing" such as this, that might make you run to the flowing streams?

—St. Augustine, *Expositions on the Psalms*

Questions to Think About
1. What do I really long for most of all?
2. How can I turn that longing toward God?

Psalm 45

This love song expresses the love of a princess for the King of Israel. But Christians also see it as an allegory of the love of the Church for Christ.

To the choirmaster: according to Lilies.
A Maskil of the Sons of Korah; a love song.

My heart overflows with a goodly theme;
I address my verses to the king;
my tongue is like the pen of a ready scribe.

You are the fairest of the sons of men;
   grace is poured upon your lips;
   therefore God has blessed you for ever.
Gird your sword upon your thigh, O mighty one,
   in your glory and majesty!

In your majesty ride forth victoriously
   for the cause of truth and to defend the right;
   let your right hand teach you dread deeds!
Your arrows are sharp
   in the heart of the king's enemies;
   the peoples fall under you.

Your divine throne endures for ever and ever.
   Your royal scepter is a scepter of equity;
   you love righteousness and hate wickedness.

Therefore God, your God, has anointed you
   with the oil of gladness above your fellows;
     your robes are all fragrant with myrrh and aloes and
       cassia.
From ivory palaces stringed instruments make you
     glad;
   daughters of kings are among your ladies of honor;
   at your right hand stands the queen in gold of
     Ophir.

Hear, O daughter, consider, and incline your ear;
   forget your people and your father's house;
   and the king will desire your beauty.
Since he is your lord, bow to him;
   the people of Tyre will sue your favor with gifts,
   the richest of the people with all kinds of wealth.

The daughter of the king is decked in her chamber
    with gold-woven robes;
   in many-colored robes she is led to the king,
   with her virgin companions, her escort, in her train.
With joy and gladness they are led along
   as they enter the palace of the king.

Instead of your fathers shall be your sons;
   you will make them princes in all the earth.
I will cause your name to be celebrated in all
    generations;
   therefore the peoples will praise you for ever and
    ever.

> **Words to Remember**
> I will cause your name to be celebrated in all
>   generations;
>   therefore the peoples will praise you for ever and
>   ever.

The God Who Anoints and Is Anointed

The common Christian interpretation of this psalm, that Jesus is the Lord's Anointed, leads St. Ambrose to the question of the Trinity: how can there be multiple Persons but only one God?

> Again, you may read in [this] psalm how the prophet not only calls the Father God but also proclaims the Son as God, saying: "Your divine throne endures for ever and ever." And further on: "God, your God, has anointed you with the oil of gladness above your fellows."
>
> This God who anoints, and God who in the flesh is anointed, is the Son of God. For what peers does Christ have in his anointing, except such as are in the flesh? You see, then, that God is anointed by God, but being anointed in taking upon him the nature of mankind, he is proclaimed the Son of God; yet the principle of the Law is not broken.
>
> So again, when you read, "The Lord rained from the Lord," acknowledge the unity of Godhead, for unity in operation does not allow of more than one individual God, even as the Lord himself has shown, saying: "Believe me, that I am in the Father, and the

Father in me: or believe me for the very works' sake." Here, too, we see that unity of Godhead is signified by unity in operation.

—St. Ambrose, *Exposition of the Christian Faith*

Questions to Think About
1. In my relationships with others, do I love others with the love that Christ has for his people? How can I grow in loving others more selflessly?
2. How can I express my own love for Christ in a way that will bring others toward him?

Psalm 51

The superscription tells us that David composed this psalm when he was at his very lowest point—when he had committed the horrible sin, not only of adultery with Bathsheba, but, worse, of sending her husband to his death—a sin that was brought home to him by the fearless prophet Nathan. If ever a man needed forgiveness, David did at that moment. The words of this psalm are used in Christian liturgies all over the world.

> *To the choirmaster.*
> *A Psalm of David, when Nathan the prophet came to him, after he had gone in to Bathsheba.*

> Have mercy on me, O God,
>   according to your merciful love;
>   according to your abundant mercy blot out my
>   transgressions.
> Wash me thoroughly from my iniquity,
>   and cleanse me from my sin!
>
> For I know my transgressions,
>   and my sin is ever before me.
> Against you, you only, have I sinned,
>   and done that which is evil in your sight,
> so that you are justified in your sentence
>   and blameless in your judgment.
> Behold, I was brought forth in iniquity,
>   and in sin did my mother conceive me.

Behold, you desire truth in the inward being;
    therefore teach me wisdom in my secret heart.
Purge me with hyssop, and I shall be clean;
    wash me, and I shall be whiter than snow.
Make me hear joy and gladness;
    let the bones which you have broken rejoice.
Hide your face from my sins,
    and blot out all my iniquities.

Create in me a clean heart, O God,
    and put a new and right spirit within me.
Cast me not away from your presence,
    and take not your holy Spirit from me.
Restore to me the joy of your salvation,
    and uphold me with a willing spirit.

Then I will teach transgressors your ways,
    and sinners will return to you.
Deliver me from bloodguilt, O God,
    O God of my salvation,
    and my tongue will sing aloud of your deliverance.

O Lord, open my lips,
    and my mouth shall show forth your praise.
For you have no delight in sacrifice;
    were I to give a burnt offering, you would not be pleased.
The sacrifice acceptable to God is a broken spirit;
    a broken and contrite heart, O God, you will not despise.

Do good to Zion in your good pleasure;
    rebuild the walls of Jerusalem,

then will you delight in right sacrifices,
> in burnt offerings and whole burnt offerings;
then bulls will be offered on your altar.

> **Words to Remember**
> Create in me a clean heart, O God,
> > and put a new and right spirit within me.
> Cast me not away from your presence,
> > and take not your holy Spirit from me.

Great Examples of Humility

St. Clement of Rome rounds up some of the great examples of humility in the Old Testament, making special note of David, and urges us to follow their example.

> Let us also imitate those who in goat-skins and sheep-skins (Hebrews 11:37) went about proclaiming the coming of Christ: I mean Elijah, Elisha, and Ezekiel among the prophets, and the others Scripture tells us about.
>
> Abraham was specially honored, and was called the friend of God; yet he, earnestly regarding the glory of God, humbly declared, "I am but dust and ashes" (Genesis 18:27).
>
> Moreover, it is written of Job, "Job was a righteous man, and blameless, truthful, God-fearing, and one that kept himself from all evil" (Job 1:1). But bringing an accusation against himself, he said, "No man is free from defilement, even if his life be but of one day" (Job 14:4–5).

Moses was called faithful in all God's house; and through him, God punished Egypt with plagues and tortures. Yet he, though thus greatly honored, did not adopt lofty language, but said, when the divine oracle came to him out of the bush, "Who am I, that you send me? I am a man of a feeble voice and a slow tongue." And again he said, "I am but as the smoke of a pot."

But what shall we say about David, to whom such testimony was borne, and of whom God said, "I have found a man after my own heart, David the son of Jesse; and in everlasting mercy have I anointed him?" Yet this very man says to God, "Have mercy on me, O God, according to thy steadfast love; according to thy abundant mercy blot out my transgressions...."

Thus the humility and godly submission of such great and illustrious men have made not only us, but also all the generations before us, better; even as many as have received his oracles in fear and truth.

And so, with so many great and glorious examples set before us, let us turn again to the practice of that peace which was our goal from the beginning; and let us look steadfastly to the Father and Creator of the universe, and hold on to his mighty and surpassingly great gifts of peace. Let us contemplate him with our understanding, and look with the eyes of our soul to his long-suffering will. Let us reflect how free from the wrath he is toward all his creation.

—St. Clement of Rome, *Lettter to the Corinthians*

Have Mercy If You Expect Mercy

St. John Chrysostom warns us that, if we pray in the words of this psalm, we must be prepared to exercise the same mercy we hope to receive.

> And how will you say, "Have mercy on me, O God, according to thy steadfast love; according to thy abundant mercy blot out my transgressions," when you yourself do not have mercy according to any great love—perhaps not even according to any little? For I am greatly ashamed, I admit, when I see many of the rich riding their golden-bitted chargers with a train of domestics clad in gold, and having couches of silver and other and more pomp, and yet when there is need to give to a poor man, becoming more beggarly than the very poorest.
>
> But what do they always say? "He has a regular allowance from the Church." And what is that to you? For you will not be saved because I give; and if the Church gives, you have not blotted out any of your own sins. For this cause do you not give, because the Church ought to give to the needy? Because the priests pray, will you never pray yourself? And because others fast, will you be continually drunken? Do you not know that God enacted almsgiving not so much for the sake of the poor as for the sake of the persons themselves who give?
>
> —St. John Chrysostom, *Homilies on First Corinthians*

Do Not Give in to Despair

If David could repent and be forgiven, says St. Augustine, so can you. Never imagine that your sin is too great for repentance: listen to Christ, and repent.

> Whoever you are who have sinned, and who hesitate to exercise penitence for your sin, despairing of your salvation, hear David groaning. Nathan the prophet has not been sent to you: David himself has been sent to you. Hear him crying, and cry with him; hear him groaning, and groan with him; hear him weeping, and mingle tears; hear him amended, and rejoice with him. If sin could not be kept away from you, do not let hope of pardon be kept away.
>
> Nathan the prophet was sent to him; observe the king's humility. He did not reject Nathan's words of admonition; he did not say, "Do you dare speak to me, a king?" An exalted king heard a prophet. Let his humble people hear Christ.
>
> —St. Augustine, *Expositions on the Psalms*

Questions to Think About
1. Is despair holding me back from confessing any hidden unrepented sins?
2. Have I shown the same mercy to others that I hope to receive?

Psalm 53

Folly is denying God; wisdom is seeking after God. Though the foolish may oppress God's people now, God will not allow them to go on forever. There will be a time of judgment—a time of terror for the fools who said there was no God, but a time of comfort and deliverance for the wise.

*To the choirmaster: according to Mahalath.
A Maskil of David.*

> The fool says in his heart,
>   "There is no God."
> They are corrupt, doing abominable iniquity;
>   there is none that does good.
>
> God looks down from heaven
>   upon the sons of men
> to see if there are any that are wise,
>   that seek after God.
>
> They have all fallen away;
>   they are all alike depraved;
> there is none that does good,
>   no, not one.
>
> Have those who work evil no understanding,
>   who eat up my people as they eat bread,
>   and do not call upon God?

There they are, in great terror,
   in terror such as has not been!
For God will scatter the bones of the ungodly;
   they will be put to shame, for God has rejected
      them.

O that deliverance for Israel would come from Zion!
   When God restores the fortunes of his people,
   Jacob will rejoice and Israel be glad.

> **Words to Remember**
> Have those who work evil no understanding,
>   who eat up my people as they eat bread,
>   and do not call upon God?

Wisdom Knows God by Reason and by Scripture

St. John of Damascus points out that even the wise pagans acknowledged the one God, and insists that even by reason alone we can know that God exists. We who have both reason and revelation have no excuse for doubt.

> That there is a God, then, is no matter of doubt to those who accept the holy Scriptures—I mean the Old Testament and the New—nor indeed to most of the Greeks. For, as we said, the knowledge of the existence of God is implanted in us by nature.
> But the wickedness of the evil one has prevailed so mightily against man's nature that it even drives some into denying the existence of God—that most

foolish and woeful pit of destruction (whose folly David, revealer of the Divine meaning, exposed when he said, "The fool says in his heart, 'There is no God'"). So the disciples of the Lord and his apostles, made wise by the Holy Spirit and working wonders in his power and grace, caught them in the net of miracles and drew them up out of the depths of ignorance to the light of the knowledge of God. In the same way their successors in grace and worth, both pastors and teachers, having received the enlightening grace of the Spirit, would enlighten, both by the power of miracles and by the word of grace, those walking in darkness and bring back the wanderers into the way.

But as for us who are not recipients either of the gift of miracles or the gift of teaching (for indeed we have rendered ourselves unworthy of these by our passion for pleasure), come, let us talk about a few of those things we have learned on this subject from the expounders of grace, calling on the Father, the Son, and the Holy Spirit.

All things that exist are either created or uncreated.

So if things are created, it follows that they are also wholly changeable. For things, whose existence originated in change, must also be subject to change, whether they perish or become something else by an act of will.

But if things are uncreated, they must in all consistency be also wholly unchangeable. For things that are opposed in the nature of their existence must also be opposed in the mode of their existence, that is to say, must have opposite properties. Then who will refuse to admit that all existing things, not only the ones we can sense, but even the very angels, are subject to change and transformation and movement of various kinds? For the things that have to do with the rational world, I mean angels and spirits and demons, are subject to changes of will, whether it is a progression or a retrogression in goodness, whether a struggle or a surrender; while the others suffer changes of generation and destruction, of increase and decrease, of quality and of movement in space. So things that are changeable are also wholly created.

But things that are created must be the work of some maker, and the maker cannot have been created. For if he had been created, he also must surely have been created by someone, and so on till we arrive at something uncreated. The Creator, then, being uncreated, is also wholly unchangeable. And what could this be other than God?

And even the very fact that creation goes on, preserved and maintained, teaches us that there is a God who supports and maintains and preserves and always provides for this universe.

For how could opposite natures, such as fire and water, air and earth, have combined with each other so as to form one complete world, and continue to abide in indissoluble union, if there were not some omnipotent power binding them together and always preserving them from dissolution?

What gave order to heaven and earth, and all those things that move in the air and in the water, or rather to what was in existence before these, namely, to heaven and earth and air and the elements of fire and water? What mingled and distributed them? What set them in motion and keeps them in their unceasing and unhindered course? Was it not the Artificer of these things, the One who has built into everything the law by which the universe is carried on and directed? Who then is the Artificer of these things? Is it not the One who created them and brought them into existence?

For we shall not attribute such a power to random chance. For, even supposing they came into being by random chance, what about the power that put it all in order? And let us grant this, if you please. What about the power that has preserved and kept them in harmony with the original laws of their existence? Clearly it is something quite distinct from random chance. And what could this be other than God?

—St. John of Damascus,
Exposition of the Orthodox Faith

Questions to Think About
1. Do I live my life as though I believe what I say about God?
2. How can others better see my belief in action by the way I live?

Psalm 54

Once again, David is in trouble, and once again he prays for deliverance. But he prays with confidence, and is already planning his sacrifice of thanksgiving.

> *To the choirmaster: with stringed instruments.*
> *A Maskil of David, when the Ziphites went and told Saul,*
>   *"David is in hiding among us."*

{ Save me, O God, by your name,
    and vindicate me by your might.
Hear my prayer, O God;
    give ear to the words of my mouth.

For insolent men have risen against me,
    ruthless men seek my life;
    they do not set God before them. *Selah*

Behold, God is my helper;
    the Lord is the upholder of my life.
He will requite my enemies with evil;
    in your faithfulness put an end to them.

With a freewill offering I will sacrifice to you;
    I will give thanks to your name, O Lord, for it is good.
For you have delivered me from every trouble,
    and my eye has looked in triumph on my enemies.

> **Words to Remember**
> Save me, O God, by thy name,
> and vindicate me by thy might.
> Hear my prayer, O God;
> give ear to the words of my mouth.

The Servant Prays for Righteous Judgment

St. Hilary of Poitiers interprets the suffering of David as the suffering of Christ, the Son of David. His interpretation is typical of early Christianity; the Christians saw Christ throughout the Old Testament, but nowhere more than in the psalms. In this psalm, Hilary says, Christ, as man, prays for what is rightfully his as God.

> The suffering of the prophet David is, as we said about the title, a type of the passion of our God and Lord Jesus Christ. This is why his prayer also corresponds in meaning with the prayer of Christ, who, being the Word, was made flesh. He suffered all things like a man. In everything he said, he spoke like a man. And he who bore the infirmities and took on him the sins of men approached God in prayer with the humility proper to men.
>
> This interpretation, even though we are unwilling and slow to receive it, is required by the meaning and force of the words. There can be no doubt that everything in the psalm is uttered by David as his mouthpiece. For he says, "Save me, O God, by your name." Thus, using the words of his own prophet, the only-begotten Son of God prays in bodily humil-

iation—the Son who at the same time was claiming again the glory he had possessed before the ages. He asks to be saved by the Name of God, by which he was called and in which he was begotten, in order that the Name of God, which rightly belonged to his former nature and kind, might save him in that body in which he had been born.

So this whole passage is the utterance of one in the form of a servant—of a servant obedient unto the death of the cross, which he took upon himself and for which he prays the saving help of the Name that belongs to God, sure of salvation by that Name. Because of that, he immediately adds: "and judge me by your power."

For now as the reward for his humility in emptying himself and assuming the form of a servant, in the same humility in which he had assumed it, he was asking to resume the form he shared with God. He had saved that humanity in which as God he had obediently condescended to be born, so that humanity could bear the Name of God. And to teach us that this Name by which he prayed to be saved is more than an empty title, he prays to be judged by the power of God.

For a right reward is the essential result of judgment, as the Scripture says: "Becoming obedient unto death, yea, the death of the cross. Wherefore also God highly exalted him and gave unto him the name which is above every name." Thus, first of all, the name which is above every name is given unto him; then next, this is a judgment of decisive force, because by the power of God, he, who after being God had died as man, rose again from death as man to be God, as the Apostle says: "He was crucified from weakness, yet he lives by the power of God" (2 Corinthians 13:4), and again: "For I am not ashamed of the gospel: for it is the power of God unto salvation to every one that believes" (Romans 1:16).

For by the power of the judgment, human weakness is rescued to bear God's name and nature. Thus, as the reward for his obedience, he is exalted by the power of this judgment into the saving protection of God's name; so that he possesses both the Name and the power of God.

Again, if the prophet had begun this utterance in the way men generally speak, he would have asked to be judged by mercy or kindness, not by power. But judgment by power was a necessity in the case of one who being the Son of God was born of a virgin to be Son of Man, and who now being Son of Man was to have the Name and power of the Son of God restored to him by the power of judgment.

—St. Hilary of Poitiers, *Homilies on the Psalms*

Questions to Think About
1. How often do I pray with complete confidence that God will answer my prayer? What obstacles might keep me from praying with such confidence?
2. Do I remember to thank God when my prayers are answered—or even before?

Psalm 58

This is a prayer for God's just judgment against the proud and wicked who oppress his people. We modern Christians tend to be uncomfortable with the idea of judgment, but we have to make the distinction between our judgment and God's judgment. Our judgment is invariably adulterated with emotion and partiality; God's judgment is pure justice. Only God knows all the circumstances, even the ones hidden in people's hearts. God's "vengeance" is actually the discipline of a Father who wants what is good for us. Sometimes he has to raise his voice to get our attention.

> *To the choirmaster: according to Do Not Destroy.*
> *A Miktam of David.*

Do you indeed decree what is right, you gods?
    Do you judge the sons of men uprightly?
No, in your hearts you devise wrongs;
    your hands deal out violence on earth.

The wicked go astray from the womb,
    they err from their birth, speaking lies.
They have venom like the venom of a serpent,
    like the deaf adder that stops its ear,
so that it does not hear the voice of charmers
    or of the cunning enchanter.

O God, break the teeth in their mouths;
    tear out the fangs of the young lions, O Lord!

Let them vanish like water that runs away;
  like grass let them be trodden down and wither.
Let them be like the snail which dissolves into slime,
  like the untimely birth that never sees the sun.
Sooner than your pots can feel the heat of thorns,
  whether green or ablaze, may he sweep them away!

The righteous will rejoice when he sees the vengeance;
  he will bathe his feet in the blood of the wicked.
Men will say, "Surely there is a reward for the righteous;
  surely there is a God who judges on earth."

> **Words to Remember**
> The wicked go astray from the womb,
>   they err from their birth, speaking lies.

The Death of One Is the Life of Another

What does it mean to bathe our feet in the blood of the wicked? St. Augustine says that when we view the punishment of sinners, it should motivate us to purge ourselves from sin.

> As yet the punishments of the lower places have not come; as yet fire everlasting has not come. Let anyone who is growing in God compare himself now with an ungodly man, a blind heart with an enlightened heart. Compare two men, one seeing and one not seeing in the flesh. Is vision of the flesh such a great thing? Did Tobit have fleshly eyes at all? His own son had, and he did not; and a blind man showed a seeing man the way of life. Therefore when you see

that punishment, rejoice, because you are not in it.

Thus Scripture says, "The righteous will rejoice when he sees the vengeance." Not the punishment to come; for see what follows: "he will bathe his feet in the blood of the wicked."

What does this mean? Let your love listen. When murderers are executed, should innocent men actually go there and wash their feet? But what does it mean, "He will bathe his feet in the blood of the wicked"?

When a just man sees the punishment of a sinner, he grows himself; and the death of one is the life of another. For if spiritually blood runs from those that within are dead, you, seeing such vengeance, should wash your feet in it: live a cleaner life in the future.

And how shall a man wash his feet if he is just? For what does he have on his feet to be washed, if he is just? "But the just man of faith shall live."

Just men, therefore, he has called believers: and from the time you first believed, at once you began to be called just. For a remission of sins has been made. Even if you have some sins in the remaining part of your life—and they cannot help flowing in, like water from the sea into the hold—nevertheless, because you believed, when you see him who is completely turned away from God slain in that blindness, with fire falling on him so that he cannot see the sun, then you, who now through faith see Christ, observe the ungodly man dying, and purge yourself from sins, so that you may see Christ in substance—for the just man lives by faith. So, in a manner of speaking, you bathe your feet in the blood of the sinner.

—St. Augustine, *Expositions on the Psalms*

Questions to Think About
1. How often do I find myself judging others? Do I trust in the impartiality of God's judgment enough to leave the judging to God?
2. Do I sometimes secretly envy the lifestyles of those who do not follow the Lord? How can I better embrace the life God is calling me to lead?

Psalm 67

God is the Lord not just of Israel, but of all the nations. The believer prays that everyone on earth may come to praise the glory of God.

To the choirmaster: with stringed instruments.
A Psalm. A Song.

May God be gracious to us and bless us
    and make his face to shine upon us, *Selah*
that your way may be known upon earth,
    your saving power among all nations.
Let the peoples praise you, O God;
    let all the peoples praise you!

Let the nations be glad and sing for joy,
    for you judge the peoples with equity
    and guide the nations upon earth. *Selah*
Let the peoples praise you, O God;
    let all the peoples praise you!

The earth has yielded its increase;
    God, our God, has blessed us.
God has blessed us;
    let all the ends of the earth fear him!

> **Words to Remember**
> Let the peoples praise you, O God;
> > Let all the peoples praise you!
> Let the nations be glad and sing for joy.

The Unity of the Church

Though we are citizens of many nations, St. Cyprian insists that as Christians we must praise the Lord with one voice. We do this through our unity in the Church.

> As the twelve tribes of Israel were divided, the prophet Abijah tore his garment. But because Christ's people cannot be torn, his robe, woven and united throughout, is not divided by those who possess it; undivided, united, connected, it shows the coherent concord of our people who put on Christ. By the sacrament and sign of his garment, he has declared the unity of the Church.
>
> Who, then, is so wicked and faithless, who is so insane with the madness of discord, that either he should believe that the unity of God can be divided, or should dare to tear it—the garment of the Lord—the Church of Christ? He himself in his gospel warns us, and teaches, saying, "And there shall be one flock and one shepherd" (John 10:16). And does any one believe that in one place there can be either many shepherds or many flocks?
>
> The apostle Paul, moreover, urging upon us this same unity, beseeches and exhorts, saying, "I beseech you, brethren, by the name of our Lord Jesus Christ,

that you all speak the same thing, and that there be no schisms among you; but that you be joined together in the same mind and in the same judgment" (1 Corinthians 1:10). And again he says, "Forbearing one another in love, endeavor to keep the unity of the Spirit in the bond of peace" (Ephesians 4:3).

Do you think you can stand and live if you withdraw from the Church, building for yourself other homes and a different dwelling, when it is said to Rahab (in whom the Church was prefigured), "Your father, and your mother, and your brethren, and all the house of your father, you shall gather unto you into your house; and it shall come to pass, whosoever shall go abroad beyond the door of your house, his blood shall be upon his own head"? (Joshua 2:19).

Also, the sacrament of the Passover contains nothing else in the law of the Exodus than that the lamb, which is slain in the figure of Christ, should be eaten in one house. God speaks, saying, "In one house shall you eat it; you shall not send its flesh abroad from the house" (Exodus 12:46).

The flesh of Christ, and the holy of the Lord, cannot be sent abroad, nor is there any other home to believers but the one Church. This home, this household of unanimity, the Holy Spirit designates and points out in the psalms, saying, "God, who makes men to dwell with one mind in a house." In the house of God, in the Church of Christ, men dwell with one mind, and continue in concord and simplicity.

—St. Cyprian of Carthage, *On the Unity of the Church*

Questions to Think About
1. What part might I play in helping to bring all nations to praise God?
2. In my own Christian community, how can I be a force for unity rather than division?

Psalm 70

Surrounded by enemies, David faces not only danger but insults. The great military leader confesses himself "poor and needy," and admits that he can do nothing without God's help.

To the choirmaster.
A Psalm of David, for the memorial offering.

Be pleased, O God, to deliver me!
   O Lord, make haste to help me!
Let them be put to shame and confusion
   who seek my life!
Let them be turned back and brought to dishonor
   who desire my hurt!
Let them be appalled because of their shame
   who say, "Aha, Aha!"

May all who seek you
   rejoice and be glad in you!
May those who love your salvation
   say evermore, "God is great!"
But I am poor and needy;
   hasten to me, O God!
You are my help and my deliverer;
   O Lord, do not delay!

> **Words to Remember**
> Be pleased, O God, to deliver me!
> O LORD, make haste to help me!

Of the Method of Continual Prayer

St. John Cassian recommends the words of this psalm be constantly on our lips, especially whenever we are assailed by temptations—our most vicious enemies.

> Now to put our system to work. You made a good comparison when you said it was like teaching children. For children learning the first lessons in the alphabet need copies of the letters on wax, which they can look at and imitate every day, so that they can learn to trace out the shapes with a steady hand. In the same way, we must give you the shape of this spiritual contemplation, so you can keep looking at it with all your concentration. Remember how much benefit there is in constant practice, and by practicing it, along with meditation, you can manage to climb to an even higher insight.
>
> Here is the formula of our system, and of the prayer you should be praying. Every monk, as he makes progress toward keeping God in mind all the time, should keep it constantly going through his heart, and get rid of all kinds of other thoughts. For he cannot possibly hold onto it unless he has freed himself from all bodily cares and anxieties. And since a few of those who remained among the oldest fathers gave us this formula, so we only divulge it to a very few, and to those who are really eager.

And so for keeping God constantly in mind, always have this pious formula in front of you:

> "*Be pleased, O God, to deliver me! O Lord, make haste to help me!*"

For this verse has very properly been picked out from the whole of Scripture for this purpose.

It embraces every human feeling, and can be adapted appropriately to every condition, and every attack. It calls on God's help against every danger. It includes humble and pious confession. It includes the alertness of anxiety and continual fear. It includes the thought of one's own weakness, confidence in the answer, and the assurance of a present and ever-ready help. (If you are constantly calling on your Protector, you must be certain that he is always there.) It includes the glow of love and charity. It includes a knowledge of the plots, and a dread of the enemies that hem you in day and night, and from which you confess that you cannot be set free without the aid of your Defender.

This verse is an impregnable wall for all who are suffering from attacks by demons, as well as impenetrable armor and a strong shield. It does not allow those who are in a state of moroseness and anxiety of mind, or depressed by sadness or all kinds of thoughts, to despair of saving help, as it shows that he who is invoked is always looking on at our struggles and is not far from his suppliants. It warns us who are destined for spiritual success and delight of heart that we ought not to be at all elated or puffed up by our happy condition, which it assures us cannot last without God as our protector, while it implores him to help us—not just always, but speedily.

You'll find this verse helpful and useful to every one of us, in whatever condition we may be. If you want to be helped in everything all the time, you show that you need the assistance of God not only in sorrowful or hard things, but just as much in prosperous and happy ones, so that you may be delivered from the hard times and made to continue in the happy times, since you know that in both of them human weakness is unable to endure without God's assistance....

So we must pour forth the prayer of this verse continuously, without stopping—in adversity that we may be delivered, in prosperity that we may be preserved and not puffed up. Keep this verse going through your heart all the time. Whatever work you are doing, or office you are holding, or journey you are going on, do not cease to chant this. When you are going to bed, or eating, and in the last necessities of nature, think on this. This thought in your heart may be to you a saving formula, and not only keep you unharmed by all attacks of devils, but also purify you from all faults and earthly stains, and lead you to that invisible and celestial contemplation, and carry you on to that unspeakable glow of prayer, of which so few have any experience.

When you go to sleep, you should still be thinking about this verse, till having been molded by the constant use of it, you get used to repeating it even in your sleep. When you wake, let it be the first thing to come into your mind; let it anticipate all your waking thoughts. When you get out of bed, let it send you down on your knees, and from there send you forth to all your work and business, and let it follow you about all day long.

You should think about it, as the Lawgiver commanded, "when you sit in your house, and when you walk by the way" (Deuteronomy 6:7), sleeping and waking. You should write it on the threshold and door of your mouth—place it on the walls of your house and in the recesses of your heart—so that when you fall on your knees in prayer, this may be your chant as you kneel, and when you rise up from it to go forth to all the necessary business of life, it may be your constant prayer as you stand.

—St. John Cassian, *Conferences*

Questions to Think About
1. What efforts have I made to develop good habits in my prayer life? What habits could I adopt that would lead me to a closer relationship with the Lord?
2. When temptation attacks, do I remember to pray for help right away?

Psalm 73

We look at the lives of the very rich and say to ourselves, "I wish I could live that way." If only we knew the truth! With all their wealth and power, they can never buy or steal an ounce of happiness. "They are destroyed in a moment," but the friends of God have happiness that lasts forever.

A Psalm of Asaph.

Truly God is good to the upright,
    to those who are pure in heart.
But as for me, my feet had almost stumbled,
    my steps had well nigh slipped.
For I was envious of the arrogant,
    when I saw the prosperity of the wicked.

For they have no pangs;
    their bodies are sound and sleek.
They are not in trouble as other men are;
    they are not stricken like other men.
Therefore pride is their necklace;
    violence covers them as a garment.
Their eyes swell out with fatness,
    their hearts overflow with follies.
They scoff and speak with malice;
    loftily they threaten oppression.
They set their mouths against the heavens,
    and their tongue struts through the earth.

Therefore the people turn and praise them;
   and find no fault in them.
And they say, "How can God know?
   Is there knowledge in the Most High?"
Behold, these are the wicked;
   always at ease, they increase in riches.
All in vain have I kept my heart clean
   and washed my hands in innocence.
For all the day long I have been stricken,
   and chastened every morning.

If I had said, "I will speak thus,"
   I would have been untrue to the generation of your children.
But when I thought how to understand this,
   it seemed to me a wearisome task,
until I went into the sanctuary of God;
   then I perceived their end.
Truly you set them in slippery places;
   you make them fall to ruin.
How they are destroyed in a moment,
   swept away utterly by terrors!
They are like a dream when one awakes,
   on awaking you despise their phantoms.

When my soul was embittered,
   when I was pricked in heart,
I was stupid and ignorant,
   I was like a beast toward you.
Nevertheless I am continually with you;
   you hold my right hand.
You guide me with your counsel,
   and afterward you will receive me to glory.

Whom have I in heaven but you?
>   And there is nothing upon earth that I desire
>   besides you.

My flesh and my heart may fail,
>   but God is the strength of my heart and my portion
>   for ever.

For behold, those who are far from you shall perish;
>   you put an end to those who are false to you.

But for me it is good to be near God;
>   I have made the Lord GOD my refuge,
>   that I may tell of all your works.

> **Words to Remember**
> Whom have I in heaven but you?
>   And there is nothing upon earth that I desire
>   besides you.
> My flesh and my heart may fail,
>   but God is the strength of my heart and my portion
>   for ever.

Consolation for the Death of a Friend

While St. Jerome was studying this psalm with his friend Marcella, a message arrived that their dear friend Lea had died unexpectedly. A few hours later, after he had gotten over the initial shock, Jerome wrote this letter to Marcella. He consoles her by making the same contrast that the psalm makes: between the wicked rich (a Roman consul who had just died), who have only fleeting wealth, and the virtuous poor (Lea), who have God as their refuge forever.

> Today, about the third hour, I was just beginning to read with you [this] psalm. . . . And just as I had come on the passage in which the righteous man declares, "If I had said, 'I will speak thus,' I would have been untrue to the generation of thy children," . . . suddenly the news came that our most saintly friend Lea had departed from the body.

As was only natural, you turned deadly pale; for there are few persons, if any, who do not burst into tears when the earthen vessel breaks. But if you wept it was not from doubt as to her future lot, but only because you had not rendered to her the last sad offices which are due to the dead. Finally, as we were still conversing together, a second message informed us that her remains had been already conveyed to Ostia.

You may ask what is the use of repeating all this? I will reply in the apostle's words, "much every way." . . .

Who can sufficiently eulogize our dear Lea's mode of living? So complete was her conversion to the Lord that, becoming the head of a monastery, she showed herself a true mother to the virgins in it, wore coarse sackcloth instead of soft raiment, passed sleepless nights in prayer, and instructed her companions even more by example than by precept. So great was her humility that she, who had once been the mistress of many, was known as the servant of all; and certainly, the less she was reckoned an earthly mistress the more she became a servant of Christ. She was careless of her dress, neglected her hair, and ate only the coarsest food. Still, in all that she did, she avoided ostentation that she might not have her reward in this world.

Now, therefore, in return for her short toil, Lea enjoys everlasting happiness; she is welcomed into the choirs of the angels; she is comforted in Abraham's bosom. And, as once the beggar Lazarus saw the rich man, for all his purple, lying in torment, so does Lea see the consul, not now in his triumphal robe but clothed in mourning, and asking for a drop of water from her little finger.

How great a change have we here! A few days ago the highest dignitaries of the city walked before him as he ascended the ramparts of the capitol like a general celebrating a triumph; the Roman people leapt up to welcome and applaud him, and at the news of his death the whole city was moved. Now he is desolate and naked, a prisoner in the foulest darkness, and not, as his unhappy wife falsely asserts, set in the royal abode of the milky way. On the other hand Lea, who was always shut up in her one closet, who seemed poor and of little worth, and whose life was accounted madness, now follows Christ and sings, "Like as we have heard, so have we seen in the city of our God."

And now for the moral of all this, which, with tears and groans, I beg you to remember. While we run the way of this world, we must not clothe ourselves with two coats, that is, with a twofold faith, or burden ourselves with leather shoes, that is, with dead works; we must not allow pockets full of money to weigh us down, or lean upon the staff of worldly power. We must not seek to possess both Christ and the world. No; things eternal must take the place of things transitory; and since, physically speaking, we daily anticipate death, if we wish for immortality we must realize that we are but mortal.

—St. Jerome, *Letters*

Questions to Think About
1. Have I put too much of my faith in the temporary things of this earth?
2. What would it mean in my life to let things eternal take the place of things transitory?

Psalm 78

This long poem tells the complete sacred history of Israel, from the Exodus through the Assyrian conquest of the northern kingdom. The theme is, in some ways, the theme of the whole Old Testament. When Israel is faithful, God sends prosperity; when Israel turns away, God sends judgment.

A Maskil of Asaph.

Give ear, O my people, to my teaching;
    incline your ears to the words of my mouth!
I will open my mouth in a parable;
    I will utter dark sayings from of old,
things that we have heard and known,
    that our fathers have told us.
We will not hide them from their children,
    but tell to the coming generation
the glorious deeds of the LORD, and his might,
    and the wonders which he has wrought.

He established a testimony in Jacob,
    and appointed a law in Israel,
which he commanded our fathers
    to teach to their children;
that the next generation might know them,
    the children yet unborn,
and arise and tell them to their children,
    so that they should set their hope in God,
and not forget the works of God,

>   but keep his commandments;
> and that they should not be like their fathers,
>   a stubborn and rebellious generation,
> a generation whose heart was not steadfast,
>   whose spirit was not faithful to God.
>
> The Ephraimites, armed with the bow,
>   turned back on the day of battle.
> They did not keep God's covenant,
>   but refused to walk according to his law.
> They forgot what he had done,
>   and the miracles that he had shown them.
> In the sight of their fathers he wrought marvels
>   in the land of Egypt, in the fields of Zoan.
> He divided the sea and let them pass through it,
>   and made the waters stand like a heap.
> In the daytime he led them with a cloud,
>   and all the night with a fiery light.
> He cleft rocks in the wilderness,
>   and gave them drink abundantly as from the deep.
> He made streams come out of the rock,
>   and caused waters to flow down like rivers.
>
> Yet they sinned still more against him,
>   rebelling against the Most High in the desert.
> They tested God in their heart
>   by demanding the food they craved.
> They spoke against God, saying,
>   "Can God spread a table in the wilderness?
> He smote the rock so that water gushed out
>   and streams overflowed.
> Can he also give bread,
>   or provide meat for his people?"

Therefore, when the LORD heard, he was full of wrath;
  a fire was kindled against Jacob,
    his anger mounted against Israel;
because they had no faith in God,
  and did not trust his saving power.
Yet he commanded the skies above,
  and opened the doors of heaven;
and he rained down upon them manna to eat,
  and gave them the grain of heaven.
Man ate of the bread of the angels;
  he sent them food in abundance.
He caused the east wind to blow in the heavens,
  and by his power he led out the south wind;
he rained flesh upon them like dust,
  winged birds like the sand of the seas;
he let them fall in the midst of their camp,
  all around their habitations.
And they ate and were well filled,
  for he gave them what they craved.
But before they had sated their craving,
  while the food was still in their mouths,
the anger of God rose against them
  and he slew the strongest of them,
  and laid low the picked men of Israel.

In spite of all this they still sinned;
  despite his wonders they did not believe.
So he made their days vanish like a breath,
  and their years in terror.
When he slew them, they sought for him;
  they repented and sought God earnestly.
They remembered that God was their rock,
  the Most High God their redeemer.

But they flattered him with their mouths;
   they lied to him with their tongues.
Their heart was not steadfast toward him;
   they were not true to his covenant.
Yet he, being compassionate,
   forgave their iniquity,
   and did not destroy them;
he restrained his anger often,
   and did not stir up all his wrath.
He remembered that they were but flesh,
   a wind that passes and comes not again.
How often they rebelled against him in the wilderness
   and grieved him in the desert!
They tested him again and again,
   and provoked the Holy One of Israel.
They did not keep in mind his power,
   or the day when he redeemed them from the foe;
when he wrought his signs in Egypt,
   and his miracles in the fields of Zoan.
He turned their rivers to blood,
   so that they could not drink of their streams.
He sent among them swarms of flies, which devoured them,
   and frogs, which destroyed them.
He gave their crops to the caterpillar,
   and the fruit of their labor to the locust.
He destroyed their vines with hail,
   and their sycamores with frost.
He gave over their cattle to the hail,
   and their flocks to thunderbolts.
He let loose on them his fierce anger,
   wrath, indignation, and distress,
   a company of destroying angels.

He made a path for his anger;
> he did not spare them from death,
> but gave their lives over to the plague.
He smote all the first-born in Egypt,
> the first issue of their strength in the tents of Ham.
Then he led forth his people like sheep,
> and guided them in the wilderness like a flock.
He led them in safety, so that they were not afraid;
> but the sea overwhelmed their enemies.
And he brought them to his holy land,
> to the mountain which his right hand had won.
He drove out nations before them;
> he apportioned them for a possession
> and settled the tribes of Israel in their tents.

Yet they tested and rebelled against the Most High God,
> and did not observe his testimonies,
but turned away and acted treacherously like their fathers;
> they twisted like a deceitful bow.
For they provoked him to anger with their high places;
> they moved him to jealousy with their graven images.
When God heard, he was full of wrath,
> and he utterly rejected Israel.
He forsook his dwelling at Shiloh,
> the tent where he dwelt among men,
and delivered his power to captivity,
> his glory to the hand of the foe.
He gave his people over to the sword,
> and vented his wrath on his heritage.

Fire devoured their young men,
   and their maidens had no marriage song.
Their priests fell by the sword,
   and their widows made no lamentation.
Then the Lord awoke as from sleep,
   like a strong man shouting because of wine.
And he put his adversaries to rout;
   he put them to everlasting shame.

He rejected the tent of Joseph,
   he did not choose the tribe of Ephraim;
but he chose the tribe of Judah,
   Mount Zion, which he loves.
He built his sanctuary like the high heavens,
   like the earth, which he has founded for ever.
He chose David his servant,
   and took him from the sheepfolds;
from tending the ewes that had young he brought him
   to be the shepherd of Jacob his people,
   of Israel his inheritance.
With upright heart he tended them,
   and guided them with skilful hand.

Words to Remember

We will not hide them from their children,
   but tell to the coming generation
the glorious deeds of the LORD, and his might,
   and the wonders which he has wrought.

More Excellent than the Bread of Angels

The Israelites, as the psalm recalls, "ate of the bread of the angels," the manna that came from heaven. But this was only a foreshadowing of the true bread from heaven, the Body of Christ, which is given to us in the Eucharist.

> Now consider whether the bread of angels is more excellent or the flesh of Christ, which is indeed the body of life. That older manna came from heaven, this new manna is above the heavens; that was from heaven, this is from the Lord of the heavens; that was liable to corruption if kept a second day, this is far from all corruption—for whosoever shall taste it worthily shall not be able to feel corruption. For them water flowed from the rock, for you Blood flowed from Christ; water satisfied them for a time, the Blood satiates you for eternity. The Hebrew drinks and thirsts again, you after drinking will be beyond the power of thirsting; that was in a shadow, this is in truth.
>
> If what you wonder at so much is but shadow, how great must that be whose very shadow you wonder at. What happened in the case of the fathers was shadow: "They drank, it is said, of that Rock that followed them, and that Rock was Christ. But with many of them, God was not well pleased, for they were overthrown in the wilderness. . . . Now these things were done in a figure concerning us" (1 Corinthians 10:4, 6). You recognize now which are the more excellent, for light is better than shadow, truth than a figure, the Body of its Giver than the manna from heaven.
>
> —St. Ambrose, *On the Mysteries*

Questions to Think About

1. How do the lessons of the sacred histories in the Old Testament, as this psalm expresses them, shed light on God's plan of salvation for me? For the Church?
2. When I read about the miracles of the Exodus, do I remember the greater miracle I experience at every Mass?

Psalm 82

What God asks of us in our earthly lives is simple: we must protect the poor and the needy against the proud and wicked, the weak against the strong.

A Psalm of Asaph.

God has taken his place in the divine council;
    in the midst of the angels he holds judgment:
"How long will you judge unjustly
    and show partiality to the wicked? *Selah*
Give justice to the weak and the fatherless;
    maintain the right of the afflicted and the destitute.
Rescue the weak and the needy;
    deliver them from the hand of the wicked."

They have neither knowledge nor understanding,
    they walk about in darkness;
    all the foundations of the earth are shaken.

I say, "You are gods,
    sons of the Most High, all of you;
nevertheless, you shall die like men,
    and fall like any prince."

Arise, O God, judge the earth;
    for to thee belong all the nations!

> **Words to Remember**
> Give justice to the weak and the fatherless;
>   maintain the right of the afflicted and the destitute.
> Rescue the weak and the needy;
>   deliver them from the hand of the wicked.

"You Are Gods"

St. Cyril of Jerusalem uses the psalm to illuminate the gift and mystery of baptism, which makes us children of God. The Fathers referred to this mystery as "deification" or "divinization." St. Peter said that we are made "partakers of the divine nature" (2 Peter 1:4). Jesus himself quoted this psalm in John 10:34.

> Look what a great dignity Jesus bestows on you. You were called a catechumen, while the word echoed all around you from the outside. You heard about hope, but you did not know it. You heard about mysteries, but you did not understand them. You heard the Scriptures, but you did not know the depths of them. Now the echo is no longer outside you, but inside: for the Spirit that dwells in you makes your mind a house of God from now on. When you have heard what is written about the mysteries, then you will understand things you did not know before.
>
> And do not think this is a small thing you receive. Though you are only a miserable man, you receive one of God's titles.
>
> Hear St. Paul: "God is faithful."
> Hear another Scripture: "God is faithful and just."

The psalmist foresaw that men would receive one of God's titles, and said this in the person of God: "You are gods, sons of the Most High, all of you."

But beware: do not have the title of the faithful, but the will of the faithless. You have entered a contest. Strive to the end of the race: you will never have another opportunity like this.

If your wedding day were coming up, would you not have set aside everything else, and worked on preparing for the feast? And on the eve of consecrating your soul to the heavenly Bridegroom, will you not give up the things of the flesh, so that you may win the things of the spirit?

—St. Cyril of Jerusalem, *Catechetical Lectures*

Questions to Think About

1. How do I rescue the weak and needy? What do I do to defend the powerless?
2. How often do I think of myself as a son or daughter of God? Why is it important to do so?

Psalm 85

God was merciful once; now the psalmist prays for that mercy again. The psalm ends with a confident declaration that the prayer will be answered: though things look hopeless now, God will show mercy.

To the choirmaster.
A Psalm of the Sons of Korah.

Lord, you were favorable to your land;
 you brought back the captives of Jacob.
You forgave the iniquity of your people;
 you pardoned all their sin. *Selah*
You withdrew all your wrath;
 you turned from your hot anger.

Restore us again, O God of our salvation,
 and put away your indignation toward us!
Will you be angry with us for ever?
 Will you prolong your anger to all generations?
Will you not revive us again,
 that your people may rejoice in you?
Show us your merciful love, O Lord,
 and grant us your salvation.

Let me hear what God the Lord will speak,
 for he will speak peace to his people,
 to his saints, to those who turn to him in their
  hearts.

Surely his salvation is at hand for those who fear him,
>   that glory may dwell in our land.

Mercy and faithfulness will meet;
>   righteousness and peace will kiss each other.
Faithfulness will spring up from the ground,
>   and righteousness will look down from heaven.
Yes, the Lord will give what is good,
>   and our land will yield its increase.
Righteousness will go before him,
>   and make his footsteps a way.

> **Words to Remember**
> Let me hear what God the Lord will speak,
>   for he will speak peace to his people,
>   to his saints, to those who turn to him in their
>   hearts.

Perfect Peace

What is perfect peace? Nothing earthly, says St. Augustine. Everything that brings you peace in an earthly way will kill you eventually. But there will come a time when death is swallowed up in victory, and then we will know true peace.

> "Let me hear." The prophet spoke: God spoke within him, and the world made a noise outside. Therefore he retires for a little while from the noise of the world, and turns back toward himself, and then turns from himself back to the One whose voice he heard within. He seals up his ears, as it were, against the riotous

racket of this life, and against the soul weighed down by the corruptible body, and against the imagination, which thinks about many things as the earthly tent presses down on it. Then he says, "Let me hear what God the Lord will speak."

And what did he hear? "For he will speak peace to his people."

The voice of Christ, then, the voice of God, is peace: it calls to peace. Listen! It says, whoever among you are not yet in peace, love peace: for what better can you have from me than peace?

What is peace? Where there is no war. What does that mean, "where there is no war"? Where there is no contradiction, where there is no resistance, nothing to oppose.

Are we there yet? Is there not a conflict with the devil now? Are not all the saints and faithful ones wrestling with the prince of demons?

And how do they wrestle with someone they do not see? They wrestle with their own desires, by which he suggests sins to them: and by not consenting to what he suggests, though they are not conquered, yet they fight. Therefore there is not yet peace where there is fighting. . . .

Whatever we provide for our refreshment, there again we find weariness. Are you hungry, someone asks you; you answer, I am. He places food before you for your refreshment; keep eating it, for you have need of it; yet in continuing that which you need for refreshment, you find weariness in it.

By sitting a long time, you were tired; you rise and refresh yourself by walking; continue that relief, and by much walking you are wearied; again you would sit down. Find me anything by which you are refreshed, in which—if you continue—you do not become weary again.

What peace, then, is that which men have here, opposed by so many troubles, desires, wants, wearinesses? This is no true, no perfect peace. What will be perfect peace? "This corruptible must put on incorruption, and this mortal must put on immortality" (1 Corinthians 15:53).

Keep eating and eating; this itself will kill you. Persevere in fasting much; by this you will die.

Sit continually, being resolved not to rise up; by this you will die. Keep walking and never rest; by this you will die.

Stay awake continually, taking no sleep; by this you will die. Sleep continually, never waking, thus too you will die.

When, therefore, death shall be swallowed up in victory, these things shall no longer be: there will be full and eternal peace. We shall be in a City, of which, brethren, when I speak I find it hard to leave off, especially when sins grow so common here.

Who would not long for that City from which no friend goes out, in which no enemy enters, where is no tempter, no traitor, no one dividing God's people, no one wearying the Church in the service of the devil; since the prince of all the evil ones himself is cast into eternal fire, and with him those who consent to him, and who have no will to retire from him?

There shall be peace made pure in the sons of God, all loving one another, seeing one another full of God, since God shall be all in all. We shall have God as our common object of vision, God as our common possession, God as our common peace. For whatever he gives us now, he himself will be to us instead of his gifts; this will be full and perfect peace.

This he speaks to his people: this is what he would hear who said, "Let me hear what God the Lord will speak, for he will speak peace to his people, to his saints, to those who turn to him in their hearts."

My brethren, do you wish that that peace which God speaks should belong to you? Turn your heart to him: not to me, or to him over there, or to any man. For whatever man would turn the hearts of men to himself, he falls with them. Which is better, that you *fall* with him to whom you turn yourself, or that you *stand* with him with whom you turn yourself? Our joy, our peace, our rest, the end of all troubles, is no one but God: blessed are "those who turn to him in their hearts."

—St. Augustine, *Expositions on the Psalms*

Questions to Think About
1. Do I have enough faith in God's mercy to ask for it even when I've sinned *again*?
2. When I need peace and relaxation, how often do I turn to prayer?

Psalm 94

More than one psalm invokes the righteous vengeance of God on his enemies. These psalms tend to make us very uncomfortable today. In the light of Christ, we know that we are supposed to turn the other cheek. But God, whose judgment is perfect, "knows the thoughts of man," and will not allow evil to triumph.

{ O Lord, you God of vengeance,
>   you God of vengeance, shine forth!
> Rise up, O judge of the earth;
>   render to the proud their deserts!
> O Lord, how long shall the wicked,
>   how long shall the wicked exult?

They pour out their arrogant words,
   they boast, all the evildoers.
They crush your people, O Lord,
   and afflict your heritage.
They slay the widow and the sojourner,
   and murder the fatherless;
and they say, "The Lord does not see;
   the God of Jacob does not perceive."

Understand, O dullest of the people!
   Fools, when will you be wise?
He who planted the ear, does he not hear?
He who formed the eye, does he not see?
He who chastens the nations, does he not chastise?

He who teaches men knowledge,
    the Lord, knows the thoughts of man,
    that they are but a breath.

Blessed is the man whom you chasten, O Lord,
    and whom you teach out of thy law
to give him respite from days of trouble,
    until a pit is dug for the wicked.
For the Lord will not forsake his people;
    he will not abandon his heritage;
for justice will return to the righteous,
    and all the upright in heart will follow it.

Who rises up for me against the wicked?
    Who stands up for me against evildoers?
If the Lord had not been my help,
    my soul would soon have dwelt in the land of silence.
When I thought, "My foot slips,"
    thy steadfast love, O Lord, held me up.
When the cares of my heart are many,
    thy consolations cheer my soul.
Can wicked rulers be allied with thee,
    who frame mischief by statute?
They band together against the life of the righteous,
    and condemn the innocent to death.
But the Lord has become my stronghold,
    and my God the rock of my refuge.
He will bring back on them their iniquity
    and wipe them out for their wickedness;
the Lord our God will wipe them out.

> **Words to Remember**
> Blessed is the man whom you chasten, O Lord,
>   and whom you teach out of your law.

The Righteous Judgment of God

We sometimes despair when we see the wicked apparently prospering, with no punishment coming to them. Why doesn't God punish the people who make us suffer? St. Augustine tells us that we should instead be thankful that God is so indulgent. We should be careful when we wish for punishment, or it might come to us.

> As we listened with much attention while the psalm was in reading, so let us listen attentively while the Lord reveals the mysteries which he has deigned to obscure in this passage.
>
> For some mysteries in the Scriptures are shut up for this reason, not that they may be denied, but that they may be opened to those who knock. If therefore you knock with pious feeling and sincere heartfelt love, God, who sees from what motives you knock, will open to you.
>
> We all know that many (and I wish we may not be among their number) murmur against God's longsuffering, and grieve either that impious and wicked men live in this world, or that they have great power; and what is more, that the bad generally have great power against the good, and that the bad often oppress the good; that the wicked exult, while the good suffer; the evil are proud, while the good are humbled.

Observing such things in the human race (for they abound), impatient and weak minds are perverted, as if they were good in vain; since God turns his eyes away, or seems to turn them away, from the good works of the pious and faithful, and to promote the wicked in those pleasures which they love.

Weak men, therefore, imagining that they live well in vain, are induced to imitate the wickedness of those whom they see flourishing. Or bodily or mental weakness may hold them back, because they are afraid of the penal laws of the world—not because they love justice, but, to speak more openly, fearing the condemnation of men among men. But even if they refrain from wicked deeds, they still think wicked thoughts. And among their wicked thoughts, the chief is the wickedness that leads them impiously to imagine that God neglects and does not care about human affairs: and either that he holds the good and the wicked in equal favor, or even (and this is a still more pernicious notion) that he persecutes the good, and favors the wicked.

Whoever thinks that way, even if he does no harm to any man, does the greatest harm to himself, and is impious against himself, and by his wickedness does not hurt God, but kills himself....

Let us now listen to the psalm.

"O Lord, thou God of vengeance, thou God of vengeance, shine forth!"

Do you think that he does not punish? The "God of vengeance" does punish. What does "God of vengeance" mean? The God of punishments.

So you grumble because the bad are not punished. Do not grumble! You might be among those who are punished.

That man stole something, and lives: you grumble against God, because he who stole something from you does not die. ... Therefore, if you would have another correct his hand, you must first correct your tongue. You would have him correct his heart toward man; correct your heart toward God. Otherwise, when you desire the vengeance of God, if it *does* come, it might find you first.

For God will come: he will come, and will judge those who continue in their wickedness, ungrateful for the prolongation of his mercy, for his longsuffering, treasuring up for themselves wrath against the day of wrath and revelation of the righteous judgment of God, who will render to every man according to his deeds: because the Lord is the "God of vengeance," and therefore he *will* "shine forth."

Then do not grumble against God, who seems to spare the wicked; but be good, and perhaps for a short time he may *not* spare you the rod, that he may, in the end, spare you in judgment.

—St. Augustine, *Expositions on the Psalms*

Questions to Think About

1. Do I ever wonder why I don't see God's judgment against people who have injured me or others? How could God change my heart to become more forgiving?

2. When life gets difficult, how might I see past the difficulties to how God might be forming and shaping me through them?

Psalm 100

This is a psalm of thanksgiving that expresses in poetry the spontaneous outpouring of joy we feel when we see that God has answered our prayers.

A Psalm for the thank offering.

Make a joyful noise to the Lord, all the lands!
    Serve the Lord with gladness!
    Come into his presence with singing!

Know that the Lord is God!
    It is he that made us, and we are his;
    we are his people, and the sheep of his pasture.

Enter his gates with thanksgiving,
    and his courts with praise!
    Give thanks to him, bless his name!

For the Lord is good;
    his steadfast love endures for ever,
    and his faithfulness to all generations.

Words to Remember
Make a joyful noise to the Lord, all the lands!
    Serve the Lord with gladness!
    Come into his presence with singing!

Make a Joyful Noise

If we truly understand our faith, St. Methodius tells us, then we should know that joy is always the appropriate response.

☙ Come then, everyone, and let us rejoice in the Lord. Come, all you people, and let us clap our hands, and make a joyful noise to God our Savior, with the voice of melody. Let no one be without a part in this grace; let no one come short of this calling; for the seed of the disobedient is appointed to destruction. Let no one neglect to meet the King, or he might be shut out from the Bridegroom's chamber. Let no one amongst us be found to receive him with a sad countenance, or he might be condemned with those wicked citizens—the citizens, I mean, who refused to receive the Lord as King over them (Luke 19:27).

Let us all come together cheerfully; let us all receive him gladly, and hold our feast with all honesty. Instead of our garments, let us strew our hearts before him. In psalms and hymns, let us raise to him our shouts of thanksgiving; and, without ceasing, let us exclaim, "Blessed is he that comes in the name of the Lord"; for blessed are they that bless him, and cursed are they that curse him (Genesis 27:29).

Again I will say it, nor will I cease exhorting you to good: Come, beloved, let us bless him who is blessed, that we may be ourselves blessed by him. This discourse summons every age and condition to praise the Lord: kings of the earth, and all people; princes, and all judges of the earth; both young men and maidens [and raise] to God with thankful confession the hymn

God taught them, as Moses sang it before to the people when they came forth out of Egypt—namely, "Blessed is he that comes in the name of the Lord."

—St. Methodius of Olympus, *Oration on the Psalms*

> **Questions to Think About**
> 1. Do I, like the psalmist, recognize the connection between gratitude and joy?
> 2. Do I leave people happier for having talked with me?

Psalm 102

Even when life seems hopeless, the faithful believer knows that God has not abandoned him. The psalmist pours out the distress in his heart, but still expresses confidence that God will show his mercy.

A prayer of one afflicted, when he is faint and pours out his complaint before the Lord.

Hear my prayer, O Lord;
    let my cry come to you!
Do not hide your face from me
    in the day of my distress!
Incline your ear to me;
    answer me speedily in the day when I call!

For my days pass away like smoke,
    and my bones burn like a furnace.
My heart is struck down like grass, and withered;
    I forget to eat my bread.
Because of my loud groaning
    my bones cleave to my flesh.
I am like a vulture of the wilderness,
    like an owl of the waste places;
I lie awake,
    I am like a lonely bird on the housetop.
All the day my enemies taunt me,
    those who deride me use my name for a curse.
For I eat ashes like bread,

and mingle tears with my drink,
because of your indignation and anger;
   for you have taken me up and thrown me away.
My days are like an evening shadow;
   I wither away like grass.

But you, O Lord, are enthroned for ever;
   your name endures to all generations.
You will arise and have pity on Zion;
   it is the time to favor her;
   the appointed time has come.
For your servants hold her stones dear,
   and have pity on her dust.
The nations will fear the name of the Lord,
   and all the kings of the earth your glory.
For the Lord will build up Zion,
   he will appear in his glory;
he will regard the prayer of the destitute,
   and will not despise their supplication.

Let this be recorded for a generation to come,
   so that a people yet unborn may praise the Lord:
that he looked down from his holy height,
   from heaven the Lord looked at the earth,
to hear the groans of the prisoners,
   to set free those who were doomed to die;
that men may declare in Zion the name of the Lord,
   and in Jerusalem his praise,
when peoples gather together,
   and kingdoms, to worship the Lord.

He has broken my strength in mid-course;
   he has shortened my days.

"O my God," I say, "do not take me from here
   in the midst of my days,
you whose years endure
   throughout all generations!"

Of old you laid the foundation of the earth,
   and the heavens are the work of thy hands.
They will perish, but thou dost endure;
   they will all wear out like a garment.
You change them like clothing, and they pass away;
   but you are the same, and your years have no end.
The children of your servants shall dwell secure;
   their posterity shall be established before you.

> **Words to Remember**
> Hear my prayer, O Lord;
>   let my cry come to you!
> Do not hide your face from me
>   in the day of my distress!

Accept Death, but Do Not Seek It

We are mortal in our flesh, and it's good for us to keep that in mind. That's not morbid, just realistic. Yet we should not seek death, says St. Athanasius. And he goes further than that, acknowledging the natural human aversion to death and explaining that that, too, has a providential purpose.

> Now as these things are written in the Scriptures, the case is clear. The saints know that a certain time is measured out to everyone. But no one knows the end

of that time, and that is plainly indicated by David's words: "Declare unto me the shortness of my days" (Psalm 102:23 in the Greek Septuagint). He wanted to be told something he did not know. In the same way, the rich man, too, while he thought he had a long time left to live, heard the words, "Fool! This night your soul is required of you; and the things you have prepared, whose will they be?" (Luke 12:20). And the Preacher speaks confidently in the Holy Spirit, and says, "man does not know his time" (Ecclesiastes 9:12). This is why the Patriarch Isaac said to his son Esau, "Behold, I am old; I do not know the day of my death" (Genesis 27:2).

And so with Our Lord: as God and the Word of the Father, he knew the time measured out by him to all, and he was conscious of the time for suffering, which he himself had appointed also for his own body. Yet since he was made man for our sakes, he hid himself when he was sought after before that time came, as we do. When he was persecuted, he fled; and avoiding the schemes of his enemies he passed by, and "But passing through the midst of them he went away" (Luke 4:30). But when he had brought on the moment that he himself had appointed, when he desired to suffer bodily for all, he announces it to the Father, saying, "Father, the hour has come; glorify thy Son" (John 17:1). And then he no longer hid himself from those who sought him, but stood willing to be taken by them; for the Scripture says, He said to them that came unto Him, "Whom do you seek?" (John 18:4–5). and when they answered, "Jesus of Nazareth," he said to them, "I am he whom you seek." And he did this even more than once; and so they immediately led him away to Pilate. He never allowed himself to be taken before the time came, nor did he hide himself when it was come; but gave himself up to those conspired against him, so that he might show to all men that the life and death of mankind depend upon the divine sentence; and that without our Father in heaven, neither a hair of man's head can become white or black, nor a sparrow ever fall into the snare.

Our Lord thus offered himself for all; and the saints have received this example from their Savior (for even those before his coming were following his teaching!). In their conflicts with their persecutors they acted legitimately in running away and hiding themselves when they were sought after. And since they were humanly ignorant of the end of the time that Providence had appointed for them, they were unwilling to deliver themselves up into the power of those who conspired against them. But knowing on the other hand what is written, that man's portions are in God's hands, and that "the Lord kills" (1 Samuel 2:6), and the Lord "brings to life," they preferred to endure unto the end, going about, as the Apostle has said, "in skins of sheep and goats, destitute, afflicted, ill-treated, of whom the world was not worthy—wandering over deserts and mountains, and in dens and caves of the earth (Hebrews 11:27–28). They did this until either the appointed time of death arrived, or God who had appointed their time spoke to them and stopped the schemes of their enemies, or delivered the persecuted to their persecutors.

—St. Athanasius, *In Defense of His Flight*

Questions to Think About
1. Do I have a healthy, Christian sense of my own mortality? Do I make an effort to see my life in light of its earthly end?
2. When I'm sick or in trouble, can I still summon the confidence to praise God? How might reading Scripture, going to Mass, or praying with a friend help?

Psalm 104

There is no more glorious hymn to the beauty and majesty of creation than this psalm. With its catalog of wonders, from the grass to the monstrous leviathan, the psalm celebrates the world God has made and the relationship between the Creator and the created.

Bless the Lord, O my soul!
    O Lord my God, thou art very great!
You are clothed with honor and majesty,
    who cover yourself with light as with a garment,
who have stretched out the heavens like a tent,
    who have laid the beams of your chambers on the
        waters,
who make the clouds your chariot,
    who ride on the wings of the wind,
who make the winds your messengers,
    fire and flame your ministers.

You set the earth on its foundations,
    so that it should never be shaken.
You covered it with the deep as with a garment;
    the waters stood above the mountains.
At your rebuke they fled;
    at the sound of your thunder they took to flight.
The mountains rose, the valleys sank down
    to the place which you appointed for them.
You set a bound which they should not pass,
    so that they might not again cover the earth.

You make springs gush forth in the valleys;
> they flow between the hills,
they give drink to every beast of the field;
> the wild donkeys quench their thirst.
By them the birds of the air have their habitation;
> they sing among the branches.
From your lofty abode you water the mountains;
> the earth is satisfied with the fruit of your work.

You cause the grass to grow for the cattle,
> and plants for man to cultivate,
that he may bring forth food from the earth,
> and wine to gladden the heart of man,
oil to make his face shine,
> and bread to strengthen man's heart.
The trees of the Lord are watered abundantly,
> the cedars of Lebanon which he planted.
In them the birds build their nests;
> the stork has her home in the fir trees.
The high mountains are for the wild goats;
> the rocks are a refuge for the badgers.
Thou hast made the moon to mark the seasons;
> the sun knows its time for setting.
You make darkness, and it is night,
> when all the beasts of the forest creep forth.
The young lions roar for their prey,
> seeking their food from God.
When the sun rises, they get them away
> and lie down in their dens.
Man goes forth to his work
> and to his labor until the evening.

O Lord, how manifold are thy works!
  In wisdom hast thou made them all;
  the earth is full of thy creatures.
Yonder is the sea, great and wide,
  which teems with things innumerable,
  living things both small and great.
There go the ships,
  and Leviathan which you formed to sport in it.

These all look to you,
  to give them their food in due season.
When you give to them, they gather it up;
  when you open your hand, they are filled with good
    things.
When you hide your face, they are dismayed;
  when you take away their spirit, they die
  and return to their dust.
When you send forth your Spirit, they are created;
  and you renew the face of the earth.

May the glory of the Lord endure for ever,
  may the Lord rejoice in his works,
who looks on the earth and it trembles,
  who touches the mountains and they smoke!
I will sing to the Lord as long as I live;
  I will sing praise to my God while I have being.
May my meditation be pleasing to him,
  for I rejoice in the Lord.
Let sinners be consumed from the earth,
  and let the wicked be no more!
Bless the Lord, O my soul!
Praise the Lord!

> **Words to Remember**
> I will sing to the Lord as long as I live;
>   I will sing praise to my God while I have being.
> May my meditation be pleasing to him,
>   for I rejoice in the Lord.

The Invisible Creation

The psalm recounts the glories of the visible creation, but also hints at the greater glories of the creation we can't see. St. John Damascene, the champion of religious art against the iconoclasts, develops that idea into an exploration of the nature of angels.

> He is himself the Maker and Creator of the angels: for he brought them out of nothing into being and created them after his own image, an incorporeal race, a sort of spirit or immaterial fire: in the words of the divine David, "who makest the winds thy messengers, fire and flame thy ministers." He has described their lightness and the ardor, and heat, and keenness, and sharpness with which they hunger for God and serve him, and how they are borne to the regions above and are quite delivered from all material thought.
>
> An angel, then, is an intelligent essence, in perpetual motion, with free will, incorporeal, ministering to God, having obtained by grace an immortal nature: and the Creator alone knows the form and limitation of its essence. But all that we can understand is, that it is incorporeal and immaterial. For all that is compared with God, who alone is incomparable, we find

to be dense and material. For in reality only the Deity is immaterial and incorporeal.

The angel's nature then is rational, and intelligent, and endowed with free will, changeable in will, or fickle. For all that is created is changeable, and only that which is uncreated is unchangeable. And all that is rational is endowed with free will. So because the angel's nature is rational and intelligent, it is endowed with free will: and because it is created, it is changeable, having power either to abide or progress in goodness, or to turn toward evil. . . .

Through the Word, therefore, all the angels were created, and through the sanctification by the Holy Spirit they were brought to perfection, sharing each in proportion to his worth and rank in brightness and grace.

—St. John of Damascus,
Exposition of the Orthodox Faith

The Spirit of Life

"The Teacher," the holy Macrina, who was sister to St. Basil and St. Gregory of Nyssa, explains to Gregory that this psalm reveals not only the doctrine of the Holy Spirit but also the truth of the Resurrection.

> First, I think, we must briefly run over the scattered proclamations of this doctrine in holy Scripture; they shall give the finishing touch to our discourse.
> Observe, then, that I can hear David, in the midst of his praises in the Divine Songs, saying at the end of the hymnody of [this] psalm, where he has taken for

his theme God's administration of the world, "When you take away their breath, they die and return to their dust. When you send forth your Spirit, they are created; and you renew the face of the ground."

He says that a power of the Spirit working in all vivifies the beings into whom it enters, and deprives those whom he abandons of their life.

Seeing, then, that the dying is declared to occur at the Spirit's departure, and the renewal of these dead ones at his appearance, and seeing moreover that in the order of the statement the death of those who are to be thus renewed comes first, we hold that in these words that mystery of the resurrection is proclaimed to the Church, and that David in the spirit of prophecy expressed this very gift which you are asking about.

—St. Macrina, quoted in St. Gregory of Nyssa,
On the Soul and the Resurrection

Questions to Think About
1. Do I take my stewardship of the world as seriously as I should? How does being a good steward show my appreciation for the wonders of God's creation?
2. In what ways could I grow more aware of the invisible creation as well as the visible creation?

Psalm 110

Not only a king but also a priest forever: this is the surprising promise God makes to his Anointed in this messianic psalm. God's people will be ruled by a mighty champion who will be both a king and high priest.

A Psalm of David.

The Lord says to my lord:
  "Sit at my right hand,
till I make your enemies your footstool."

The Lord sends forth from Zion
  your mighty scepter.
    Rule in the midst of your foes!
Your is dominion
  on the day you lead your host
  in holy splendor.
From the womb of the morning
  I begot you.
The Lord has sworn
  and will not change his mind,
"You are a priest for ever
  According to the order of Melchizedek."

The Lord is at your right hand;
  he will shatter kings on the day of his wrath.
He will execute judgment among the nations,
  filling them with corpses;

> he will shatter chiefs
>> over the wide earth.
> He will drink from the brook by the way;
>> therefore he will lift up his head.

> **Words to Remember**
> The Lord has sworn
>> and will not change his mind,
> "You are a priest for ever
>> According to the order of Melchizedek."

David's Son and David's Lord

"How can the son of David be David's lord?" Jesus stumped the teachers with this question (Matthew 22:43–44), but it doesn't stump a Christian. By human descent Jesus is the son of David, but he is also the Son of God.

> ℘ This psalm is one of those promises surely and openly prophesying our Lord and Savior Jesus Christ; so that we are utterly unable to doubt that Christ is announced in this psalm, since we are now Christians, and believe the gospel. . . .
>
> If someone says to us, "Is Christ the Son of David or not?" and we answer no, we contradict the gospel; for the Gospel of St. Matthew begins, "The book of the generation of Jesus Christ, the Son of David." The Evangelist declares that he is writing the book of the generation of Jesus Christ, the Son of David. The Jews, then, when asked by Christ whose Son they believed Christ to be, rightly answered, the Son of David. The

Gospel agrees with their answer. Not only the suspicion of the Jews, but the faith of Christians, declares this. . . .

"If then David in the spirit called him Lord, how is he his son?" The Jews were silent at this question: they found no further reply. Yet they did not seek him as the Lord, for they did not acknowledge him to be himself that Son of David.

But let us, brethren, both believe and declare: for "with the heart we believe unto righteousness: but with the mouth confession is made unto salvation." Let us believe, I say, and let us declare both the Son of David, and the Lord of David. Let us not be ashamed of the Son of David, lest we find the Lord of David angry with us. . . .

We know that Christ sits at the right hand of the Father since his resurrection from the dead and ascent into heaven. It is already done: we did not see it, but we have believed it: we have read it in the Scripture, have heard it preached, and hold it by faith. So that by the very circumstance that Christ was David's Son, he became his Lord also. For that which was born of the seed of David was so honored, that it was also the Lord of David.

You wonder at this, as if the same did not happen in human affairs. For if it should happen, that the son of any private person be made a king, will he not be his father's lord? And something even more wonderful may happen: not only that the son of a private person, by being made a king, may become his father's lord; but that the son of a layman, by being made a bishop, may become his father's father.

Christ took on human flesh. He died in the flesh.

He rose again in the same flesh. In the same flesh he ascended into heaven, and sits on the right hand of his Father. In this way—in this same flesh so honored, so brightened, so changed into a heavenly garb—he is both David's Son, and David's Lord.

—St. Augustine, *Expositions on the Psalms*

"Sit at My Right Hand"

Arguing against the heretical Arians, who denied the divinity of Christ, St. Ambrose points out that this psalm was meant to honor the Lord's Anointed, not to degrade him in any way. If sitting at the right hand of the Father implies inferiority, as the Arians argued, we might as well say that God the Father is degraded by sitting at the left hand of Christ! The most important thing to remember is that Christ, who is God, will be our Judge.

> If reasoning will not move you, at least let the plain aspect of the judgment move you! Raise your eyes to the Judge, see who it is that is seated, with whom he is seated, and where Christ sits at the right hand of the Father.
>
> If you cannot see this with your eyes, hear the words of the prophet: "The Lord says to my Lord: 'Sit at my right hand.'" The Son, therefore, sits at the right hand of the Father. Tell me now, you who insist that the things of God are to be judged of from the things of this world—say whether you think that the one who sits at the right hand is lower? Is it any dishonor to the Father that he sits at the Son's left hand? The Father honors the Son, and you make it an insult! The Father

makes this invitation as a sign of love and esteem, and you would make it an overlord's command! Christ has risen from the dead, and sits at the right hand of God.

But, you object, the Father said. Good, hear now a passage where the Father does not speak, and the Son prophesies: "Hereafter you shall see the Son of Man sitting at the right hand of power" (Matthew 26:64). He said this about taking back his own body—to him the Father said: "Sit at my right hand." If indeed you ask of the eternal abode of the Godhead, he said—when Pilate asked him whether he were the King of the Jews—"For this I was born." And so indeed the apostle shows that it is good for us to believe that Christ sits at the right hand of God, not by command, nor as a favor, but as God's most dearly beloved Son. For it is written for you: "Seek the things that are above, where Christ is, sitting at the right hand of God; savor the things that are above" (Colossians 3:2). This is what it means to savor the things that are above: to believe that Christ, in his sitting, does not obey as one who receives a command, but is honored as the well-beloved Son. It is with regard, then, to Christ's body that the Father says, "Sit at my right hand, till I make your enemies your footstool."

If, again, you seek to pervert the sense of these words, "I will make your enemies your footstool," I answer that the Father also brings to the Son those whom the Son raises up and makes alive. For "no man," says Christ, "can come to me, except the Father, who has sent me, draw him, and I will raise him up at the last day" (John 6:44). . . .

Moreover, sitting at the right hand is no preferment, nor does sitting at the left hand betoken dishonor, for there are no degrees in the Godhead, which is bound by no limits of space or time, which are the weights and measures of our puny human minds. There is no difference of love, nothing that divides the Unity.

—St. Ambrose, *Exposition of the Christian Faith*

Questions to Think About
1. What would I regret doing or not doing if I knew that tomorrow was my last day on earth?
2. How does taking part in the Eucharist enable me to exercise my common priesthood with Christ? At Mass and afterward, how can I make myself a living sacrifice to the Lord?

Psalm 118

This is a psalm of thanksgiving for God's mercy. St. Gregory brings out the consoling fact that God's mercy does not end when we die, but works upon us to prepare us to share life with him in a place where nothing impure can enter (see Revelation 21:27).

O give thanks to the Lord, for he is good;
   his mercy endures for ever!

Let Israel say,
   "His mercy endures for ever."
Let the house of Aaron say,
   "His mercy endures for ever."
Let those who fear the Lord say,
   "His mercy endures for ever."

Out of my distress I called on the Lord;
   the Lord answered me and set me free.
With the Lord on my side I do not fear.
   What can man do to me?
The Lord is on my side to help me;
   I shall look in triumph on those who hate me.

It is better to take refuge in the Lord
   than to put confidence in man.
It is better to take refuge in the Lord
   than to put confidence in princes.

All nations surrounded me;
    in the name of the Lord I cut them off!
They surrounded me, surrounded me on every side;
    in the name of the Lord I cut them off!
They surrounded me like bees,
    they blazed like a fire of thorns;
    in the name of the Lord I cut them off!
I was pushed hard, so that I was falling,
    but the Lord helped me.
The Lord is my strength and my song;
    he has become my salvation.

Listen, glad songs of victory
    in the tents of the righteous:
"The right hand of the Lord does valiantly!
    The right hand of the Lord is exalted;
    the right hand of the Lord does valiantly!"
I shall not die, but I shall live,
    and recount the deeds of the Lord.
The Lord has chastened me sorely,
    but he has not given me over to death.

Open to me the gates of righteousness,
    that I may enter through them
    and give thanks to the Lord.

This is the gate of the Lord;
    the righteous shall enter through it.

I thank you that you have answered me
    and have become my salvation.
The stone which the builders rejected
    has become the head of the corner.

This is the Lord's doing;
> it is marvelous in our eyes.
This is the day which the Lord has made;
> let us rejoice and be glad in it.
Save us, we beg you, O Lord!
> O Lord, we beg you, give us success!

Blessed be he who enters in the name of the Lord!
> We bless you from the house of the Lord.
The Lord is God,
> and he has given us light.
Bind the festal procession with branches,
> up to the horns of the altar!

You are my God, and I will give thanks to you;
> you are my God, I will extol you.

O give thanks to the Lord, for he is good;
> for his mercy endures for ever!

Words to Remember

Open to me the gates of righteousness,
> that I may enter through them
> and give thanks to the Lord.

This is the gate of the Lord;
> the righteous shall enter through it.

Love in Christ is the Gate of Righteousness

Pope St. Clement calls the Corinthian Church to repentance and a return to brotherly love, good order, and peaceful harmony.

> So let us quickly put an end to this matter; and let us fall down before the Lord, and beg him with tears, that he would mercifully be reconciled to us, and restore us to our former seemly and holy practice of brotherly love. For such conduct is the "gate of righteousness," which is set open for the attainment of life, as it is written, "Open to me the gates of righteousness, that I may enter through them and give thanks to the Lord." This is the gate of the Lord: the righteous shall enter in by it. Although many gates have been set open, yet this gate of righteousness is that gate in Christ, and blessed are all who have entered in and have set their way in holiness and righteousness, doing all things without disorder.

—Pope St. Clement, *Letter to the Corinthians*

Questions to think about
1. Do I recognize that the Church's peace must begin with my own repentance?
2. Do I recognize that concord and love are still the "gates of righteousness"?

Psalm 121

Israel—that is, all the faithful people of God—can always rely on God's protection.

A Song of Ascents.

I lift up my eyes to the hills.
    From where does my help come?
My help comes from the Lord,
    who made heaven and earth.

He will not let your foot be moved,
    he who keeps you will not slumber.
Behold, he who keeps Israel
    will neither slumber nor sleep.

The Lord is your keeper;
    the Lord is your shade
    on your right hand.
The sun shall not smite you by day,
    nor the moon by night.

The Lord will keep you from all evil;
    he will keep your life.
The Lord will keep
    your going out and your coming in
    from this time forth and for evermore.

> **Words to Remember**
> He will not let your foot be moved,
>   he who keeps you will not slumber.

The Keeper Who Will Not Slumber

If you're looking for someone to protect you, don't you want someone who will never lie down on the job? There's only one who fits that description, St. Augustine says: God, the protector of Israel, who never sleeps.

> Sing therefore what follows, if you wish to hear how you may most securely set your feet on the steps, so that you may not be fatigued in that ascent, nor stumble and fall. Pray in these words: "He will not let your foot be moved!"
>
> How are feet moved? How was the foot of him who was in Paradise moved?
>
> But first consider how the feet of him who was among the angels were moved: who, when his feet were moved, fell, and from an angel became a devil: for when his feet were moved he fell. How did he fall? He fell through pride.
>
> So nothing moves the feet, except pride: nothing moves the feet to a fall, except pride. Charity moves them to walk and to improve and to ascend; pride moves them to fall . . .
>
> Choose for yourself him who will neither sleep nor slumber, and your foot shall not be moved. God is never asleep: if you wish to have a keeper who never sleeps, choose God for your keeper. "He will not let

your foot be moved," you say. Very well: but he also says to you, "he who keeps you will not slumber."

Perhaps you were about to turn to men as your keepers, and to say, "Whom shall I find who will not sleep? What man will not slumber? Whom do I find? Where shall I go? Where shall I return?

The psalmist tells you: "He who keeps Israel will neither slumber nor sleep."

Do you wish to have a keeper who neither slumbers nor sleeps? "He who keeps Israel will neither slumber nor sleep," for Christ keeps Israel.

Then you must be Israel.

What does "Israel" mean? It is interpreted, "Seeing God." And how is God seen? First by faith; afterward by sight.

If you cannot as yet see him by sight, see him by faith ...

Who is there, who will neither slumber nor sleep? When you seek among men, you are deceived. You will never find anyone. Then do not trust in any man: every man slumbers, and will sleep. When does he slumber? When he bears the flesh of weakness. When will he sleep? When he is dead. Then do not trust in man. A mortal may slumber; he sleeps in death. Do not seek a keeper among men.

—St. Augustine, *Expositions on the Psalms*

Questions to Think About
1. Do I place my real trust in banks, armies, investments, fences, and locks—or in God? Why or why not?
2. How would my life be different if I put *more* trust in God?

Psalm 127

Solomon, to whom this psalm is attributed, was a wise and just monarch. Yet he attributes none of his success to himself, and everything to God.

> *A Song of Ascents.*
> *Of Solomon.*

Unless the Lord builds the house,
    those who build it labor in vain.
Unless the Lord watches over the city,
    the watchman stays awake in vain.
It is in vain that you rise up early
    and go late to rest,
eating the bread of anxious toil;
    for he gives to his beloved sleep.

Behold, sons are a heritage from the Lord,
    the fruit of the womb a reward.
Like arrows in the hand of a warrior
    are the sons of one's youth.
Happy is the man who has
    his quiver full of them!
He shall not be put to shame
    when he speaks with his enemies in the gate.

> **Words to Remember**
> Unless the Lord builds the house,
>   those who build it labor in vain.
> Unless the Lord watches over the city,
>   the watchman stays awake in vain.

The Lord Helps Those Who Help Themselves

Origen reminds us that, though we're right to attribute all good things to God, doing so doesn't absolve us of the responsibility to improve or defend ourselves.

> In the Book of Psalms—in the Songs of Ascents, which are ascribed to Solomon—we find this statement: "Unless the Lord builds the house, those who build it labor in vain. Unless the Lord watches over the city, the watchman stays awake in vain."
>
> By these words he certainly does not indicate that we should stop building or watching over the safekeeping of that city which is within us. But what he points out is this: that whatever is built without God, and whatever is guarded without him, is built in vain, and guarded to no purpose.
>
> For in all things that are well built and well protected, the Lord is held to be the cause either of the building or of its protection. For example, if we saw some magnificent structure and mass of splendid building reared with beautiful architectural skill, would we not be right to say that it was built not by human power but by divine help and might? And yet we would not mean that the labor and industry of

human effort were inactive, and had no effect at all.

Or again, if we were to see some city surrounded by a severe blockade of the enemy, in which threatening engines were brought against the walls, and the place hard pressed by siege machinery, and weapons, and fire, and all the instruments of war, ready to destroy it, would we not be right to say, if the enemy were repelled and put to flight, that the deliverance had been wrought for the liberated city by God? And yet, if we said that, we would not mean that either the vigilance of the sentinels, or the alertness of the young men, or the protection of the guards, had been wanting.

—Origen, *On First Principles*

Questions to Think About
1. When I've succeeded in something important, do I attribute my success to God?
2. Do I put all the effort I should into my daily work? What obstacles might I need to overcome to put my whole heart into my work?

Psalm 131[1]

David reminds us that humility—even in a king—is the proper attitude before God.

A gradual canticle of David.

Lord, my heart is not exalted:
    nor are my eyes lofty.
Neither have I walked in great matters,
    nor in wonderful things above me.
If I was not humbly minded, but exalted my soul:
    As a child that is weaned is toward his mother,
    so reward in my soul.

Let Israel hope in the Lord,
    from henceforth now and for ever.

> **Words to Remember**
> Lord, my heart is not exalted:
>   nor are my eyes lofty.

---

[1] For this psalm we use Challoner's revision of the Douay-Rheims Bible, because St. Hilary's exposition depends on a slightly different translation from the one found in the Revised Standard Version. In the numbering used by the Douay=Rheims Bible this is Psalm 130.

"Strike a Middle Course"

From this short psalm, St. Hilary of Poitiers, a bishop who came from a noble and wealthy family, spins a lesson in humility. Humility by itself is not enough: though we are humble, we must dare to let our souls reach up to what is most exalted.

> "O Lord, my heart is not exalted, neither have my eyes been lifted up."
>
> This psalm, a short one, teaches us the lesson of humility and meekness.... Of course we are bound to bear in mind in how great need our faith stands of humility when we hear the prophet thus speaking of it as equivalent to the performance of the highest works: "O Lord, my heart is not exalted." For a troubled heart is the noblest sacrifice in the eyes of God. The heart, therefore, must not be lifted up by prosperity, but humbly kept within the bounds of meekness through the fear of God.
>
> "Neither have my eyes been lifted up." The strict sense of the Greek here conveys a different meaning: "have not been lifted up" from one object to look on another. Yet the eyes must be lifted up in obedience to the prophet's words: "Lift up your eyes and see who has displayed all these things" (Isaiah 40:26). And the Lord says in the gospel: "Lift up your eyes, and look on the fields, that they are white unto harvest" (John 4:35). The eyes, then, are to be lifted up: not, however, to transfer their gaze elsewhere, but to remain fixed once for all upon that to which they have been raised.
>
> Then follows: "Neither have I walked amid great things, nor amid wonderful things that are above me."

It is most dangerous to walk amid mean things, and not to linger amid wonderful things. God's utterances are great; He himself is wonderful in the highest: how then can the psalmist pride himself as on a good work for not walking amid great and wonderful things?

It is the addition of the words "that are above me" that shows that the walking is not amid those things which men commonly regard as great and wonderful. For David, prophet and king as he was, once was humble and despised and unworthy to sit at his father's table; but he found favor with God, he was anointed to be king, he was inspired to prophesy. His kingdom did not make him haughty; he was not moved by hatreds: he loved those that persecuted him, he paid honor to his dead enemies, he spared his incestuous and murderous children. In his capacity of sovereign he was despised, in that of father he was wounded, in that of prophet he was afflicted; yet he did not call for vengeance as a prophet might, nor exact punishment as a father, nor requite insults as a sovereign.

And so he did not walk amid things great and wonderful which were above him.

Let us see what comes next: "If I was not humble-minded but have lifted up my soul."

What inconsistency on the prophet's part! He does not lift up his heart: he does lift up his soul. He does not walk amid things great and wonderful that are above him; yet his thoughts are not mean. He is exalted in mind and cast down in heart. He is humble in his own affairs: but he is not humble in his thought.

For his thought reaches to heaven, his soul is lifted up on high. But his heart, out of which proceed, according to the gospel, evil thoughts, murders, adulteries, fornications, thefts, false witness, railings (Matthew 15:19), is humble, pressed down beneath the gentle yoke of meekness.

We must strike a middle course, then, between humility and exaltation, so that we may be humble in heart but lifted up in soul and thought.

Then he goes on: "Like a weaned child upon his mother's breast, so will you reward my soul."

We are told that when Isaac was weaned Abraham made a feast because, now that he was weaned, he was on the verge of boyhood and was passing beyond milk food. The apostle feeds all that are imperfect in the faith and still babes in the things of God with the milk of knowledge. Thus to cease to need milk marks the greatest possible advance. Abraham proclaimed by a joyful feast that his son had come to stronger meat, and the apostle refuses bread to the carnal-minded and those that are babes in Christ.

And so the prophet prays that God, because he has not lifted up his heart, nor walked amid things great and wonderful that are above him, because he has not been humble-minded but did lift up his soul, may reward his soul, lying like a weaned child upon his mother: that is to say that he may be deemed worthy of the reward of the perfect, heavenly, and living bread, on the ground that by reason of his works already recorded he has now passed beyond the stage of milk.

But he does not demand this living bread from heaven for himself alone, he encourages all mankind to hope for it by saying: "Let Israel hope in the Lord from henceforth and forevermore." He sets no temporal limit to our hope, he bids our faithful expectation stretch out into infinity. We are to hope forever and ever, winning the hope of future life through the hope of our present life which we have in Christ Jesus our Lord, Who is blessed for ever and ever. Amen.

—St. Hilary of Poitiers, *Homilies on the Psalms*

Questions to Think About
1. Am I ever tempted to look down on anyone else? How would the truth of who I am before God help me to overcome this temptation?
2. How can I better remember to focus my attention on heaven rather than on earthly glories?

Psalm 134

A short song of praise, this psalm may have been sung at a nighttime liturgy.

A Song of Ascents.

Come, bless the Lord,
 all you servants of the Lord,
 who stand by night in the house of the Lord!
Lift up your hands to the holy place,
 and bless the Lord!

May the Lord bless you from Zion,
 he who made heaven and earth!

> **Words to Remember**
> Come, bless the Lord,
> all you servants of the Lord.

The Guardian Angels Sing God's Praise

Who are the "servants of the Lord who stand by night in the house of the Lord"? In his sermon on this psalm, St. Hilary of Poitiers sees these servants as the guardian angels, who always look on God's face.

> The angels of little children gaze upon the face of God every day. And these spirits have been sent forth to help the human race. If the guardian angels had not been given to us, we would be too weak to resist the many and powerful attacks of the evil spirits. For that purpose, we need help from a superior nature.
>
> We know this from the words the Lord speaks to strengthen Moses, who was trembling in fear: "My angel will go before you." That's why God has produced these spirits from his treasury, and given them to help humanity in its weakness—so that this divine aid might help us against the powers of this dark world, so that we may inherit salvation.

—St. Hilary of Poitiers, *Homilies on the Psalms*

Be One

For St. Augustine this psalm, with the psalm that precedes it, was a call to unity in the Church.

> "May the Lord bless you from Zion, he who made heaven and earth!" He exhorts many to bless, but his blessing goes forth only to one, because he makes one out of many: "how good and pleasant it is when brothers dwell in unity!" (Ps 133:1). It is a plural number, brethren, and yet singular, to dwell together as one. Let none of you say, "It's not addressed to me." Do you know whom he's talking about when he says, "the Lord bless you from Zion"? He blessed one. Be unified, and the blessing comes to you.

—St. Augustine of Hippo, *Expositions on the Psalms*

Questions to Think About

1. How often do I bless the Lord by night as well as by day—in private as well as in public? In what ways, in addition to prayer, can I "bless" the Lord?
2. How often do I ask for help from my guardian angel in those private moments?

Psalm 137

Israel is in exile in Babylon, the wicked city whose proud rulers destroyed Jerusalem. The gloating Babylonians want their Israelite minstrels to sing them songs of old Zion; the Israelites ask the Lord not to allow them to forget Jerusalem.

By the waters of Babylon, there we sat down and wept,
   when we remembered Zion.
On the willows there
   we hung up our lyres.
For there our captors
   required of us songs,
and our tormentors, mirth, saying,
   "Sing us one of the songs of Zion!"

How shall we sing the Lord's song
   in a foreign land?
If I forget you, O Jerusalem,
   let my right hand wither!
Let my tongue cleave to the roof of my mouth,
   if I do not remember you,
if I do not set Jerusalem
   above my highest joy!

Remember, O Lord, against the Edomites
   the day of Jerusalem,
how they said, "Raze it, raze it!
   Down to its foundations!"

O daughter of Babylon, you devastator!
  Happy shall he be who repays you
  with what you have done to us!
Happy shall he be who takes your little ones
  and dashes them against the rock!

> **Words to Remember**
> If I forget you, O Jerusalem,
>   let my right hand wither!
> Let my tongue cleave to the roof of my mouth,
>   if I do not remember you,
> if I do not set Jerusalem
>   above my highest joy!

Practice True Repentance

The state of sin is a Babylonian exile from the heavenly Jerusalem, which is the believer's true home even on earth. St. Ambrose warns us that we have not truly repented unless we are producing the fruits of repentance: charity, patience, and peace.

> And so no one in a state of sin ought to claim a right to the sacraments, for it is written: "You have sinned, be still." As David says in the psalm lately quoted: "On the willows there we hung up our lyres"; and again: "How shall we sing the Lord's song in a foreign land?" For if the flesh wars against the mind, and is not subject to the guidance of the Spirit, then that is a foreign land not subdued by the toil of the cultivator, and so it cannot produce the fruits of charity, patience, and peace.

It is better, then, to be still when you cannot practice the works of repentance. Otherwise, in the very acts of repentance, you might do something that afterward will need further repentance. For if it is once begun and not rightly carried out, it does not obtain the result of a first repentance and takes away the use of a later one.

—St. Ambrose, *On Repentance*

The Rock and the Offspring of Babylon

In a rousing exhortation, St. Augustine urges us to reject all sins, both small and large, venial sin and mortal sin, which he compares to the babies and adults of Babylon.

> Brothers and sisters, don't let your musical instruments rest when your work: sing "songs of Zion" to one another. Eagerly you have heard; now eagerly *do* what you have heard, if you don't want to be willows of Babylon, fed by its streams, bringing no fruit. But long for the everlasting Jerusalem: where your hope goes before, let your life follow. There we shall be with Christ. Christ now is our Head; now he rules us from above; in that city he will fold us to himself. We shall be equal to the angels of God. We would not dare to imagine this of ourselves, if the Truth did not promise it! Desire this, then, brothers and sisters. Think about it day and night. If the world shines happily on you, presume not; do not bargain willingly with your lusts. Is it a grown-up enemy? Let it be slain upon the Rock. Is it a little enemy? Let it be dashed against the Rock. Slay the grown-up ones on the Rock, and dash the little

ones against the Rock. Let the Rock conquer. Be built upon the Rock, if you don't want to be swept away by the stream, or the winds, or the rain. If you wish to be armed against temptations in this world, let longing for the everlasting Jerusalem grow and be strengthened in your hearts. Your captivity will pass away, your happiness will come; the last enemy shall be destroyed, and we shall triumph with our King, without death.

—St. Augustine, *Expositions on the Psalms*

Questions to Think About
1. Does adversity make me despair, blinding me to the possibility of true repentance?
2. Does my repentance bear real fruit—charity, patience, and peace?

Psalm 141

Often we hear David praying for deliverance from his enemies, and he often had need of deliverance during his long and arduous career. But in this psalm we get the distinct impression that David's most formidable enemy is himself. He prays that God will protect him from the evil thoughts of his own heart.

A Psalm of David.

I call upon you, O Lord; make haste to me!
    Give ear to my voice, when I call to you!
Let my prayer be counted as incense before you,
    and the lifting up of my hands as an evening
        sacrifice!

Set a guard over my mouth, O Lord,
    keep watch over the door of my lips!
Incline not my heart to any evil,
    to busy myself with wicked deeds
in company with men who work iniquity;
    and let me not eat of their dainties!

Let a good man strike or rebuke me in kindness,
    but let the oil of the wicked never anoint my head;
    for my prayer is continually against their wicked
        deeds.
When they are given over to those who shall
    condemn them,

then they shall learn that the word of the Lord is
   true.
As a rock which one cleaves and shatters on the land,
   so shall their bones be strewn at the mouth of
   Sheol.

But my eyes are toward you, O Lord God;
   in you I seek refuge; leave me not defenseless!
Keep me from the trap which they have laid for me,
   and from the snares of evildoers!
Let the wicked together fall into their own nets,
   while I escape.

> **Words to Remember**
> Let my prayer be counted as incense before you,
>   and the lifting up of my hands as an evening
>   sacrifice!

The Evening Sacrifice

St. Augustine interprets the "evening sacrifice" in this psalm as the sacrifice of Christ on the Cross.

> "Let my prayer be counted as incense before thee, and the lifting up of my hands as an evening sacrifice!"
>   Every Christian acknowledges that this is usually understood of the Head himself. For when the day was now sinking toward evening, the Lord upon the cross "laid down his life to take it again." He did not lose it against his will.
>   Still, we too are figured there. For what part of him

hung on the tree, except what he took of us? And how can it be that the Father should leave and abandon his only begotten Son, especially when he is one God with him? Yet, fixing our weakness upon the cross, where, as the apostle says, "our old man is crucified with him," he cried out in the voice of that "old man" of ours, "Why hast thou forsaken me?"

That, then, is the "evening sacrifice," the passion of the Lord, the Cross of the Lord, the offering of a salutary Victim, the whole burnt offering acceptable to God. That "evening sacrifice" produced, in his resurrection, a morning offering.

Prayer, then, purely directed from a faithful heart, rises like incense from a hallowed altar. Nothing is more delightful than the fragrance of the Lord: such fragrance let all have who believe.

"Set a guard over my mouth, O Lord, keep watch over the door of my lips!"

He did not say "the barrier," but "the door of my lips." A door is opened as well as shut. If then it is a "door," let it be both opened and shut; opened, to confession of sin; closed, to excusing sin.

—St. Augustine, *Expositions on the Psalms*

Questions to Think About
1. Do I ask for God's help in overcoming my own worst impulses? Do I have faith that God will give me victory?
2. Have I also asked for help in saying the right things and avoiding hurtful speech?

Psalm 145

The superscription calls this "a song of praise," and no more description is needed. The Lord is praised for his power and glory but even more for his love.

> *A Song of Praise.*
> *Of David.*

I will extol you, my God and King,
    and bless your name for ever and ever.
Every day I will bless you,
    and praise your name for ever and ever.
Great is the Lord, and greatly to be praised,
    and his greatness is unsearchable.

One generation shall laud your works to another,
    and shall declare your mighty acts.
On the glorious splendor of your majesty,
    and on your wondrous works, I will meditate.
Men shall proclaim the might of your awesome acts,
    and I will declare thy greatness.
They shall pour forth the fame of your abundant goodness,
    and shall sing aloud of your righteousness.

The Lord is gracious and merciful,
    slow to anger and abounding in mercy.
The Lord is good to all,
    and his compassion is over all that he has made.

All thy works shall give thanks to you, O Lord,
    and all your saints shall bless you!
They shall speak of the glory of your kingdom,
    and tell of your power,
to make known to the sons of men your mighty deeds,
    and the glorious splendor of your kingdom.
Your kingdom is an everlasting kingdom,
    and your dominion endures throughout all
        generations.

The Lord is faithful in all his words,
    and gracious in all his deeds.
The Lord upholds all who are falling,
    and raises up all who are bowed down.
The eyes of all look to you,
    and you give them their food in due season.
You open your hand,
    you satisfy the desire of every living thing.
The Lord is just in all his ways,
    and kind in all his doings.
The Lord is near to all who call upon him,
    to all who call upon him in truth.
He fulfils the desire of all who fear him,
    he also hears their cry, and saves them.
The Lord preserves all who love him;
    but all the wicked he will destroy.

My mouth will speak the praise of the Lord,
    and let all flesh bless his holy name for ever and
        ever.

> **Words to Remember**
> The Lord is gracious and merciful,
>   slow to anger and abounding in steadfast love.

The Eternal Word

Psalm 145 dwells on the everlastingness of God as one of his most glorious attributes. St. Athanasius takes the opportunity to address Arianism, one of the most disruptive heresies of the day, by refuting its central claim that God the Son is a lesser being than God the Father.

> And the words addressed to the Son in [this] psalm, "Your kingdom is an everlasting kingdom," forbid any one to imagine any time at all when the Word did not exist.
>
> For every interval in the ages is measured, and the Word is King and Maker of all the ages. Now, since no interval at all exists before him, it would be madness to say, "There was a time when the Everlasting was not," and "From nothing comes the Son."
>
> Now the Lord himself says, "I am the Truth." Not "I became the Truth," but always "*I am*": "*I am* the Shepherd"—"*I am* the Light"—and again, "Do you not call me, Lord and Master? And you call me well, for so *I am*." So, hearing such language from God, and the Wisdom, and Word of the Father, speaking of himself, who will hesitate any longer about the truth, and not immediately believe that the phrase "*I am*" means that the Son is eternal and without beginning?
>
> —St. Athanasius, *First Discourse Against the Arians*

Praise God!

The psalmist tells us to praise God not just with our souls, but with our bodies too. Theodoret of Cyrus sees this as a foreshadowing of the Incarnation.

> We have confessed that God the Word took not a body only but also a soul. Why then did the divine Evangelist omit in this place mention of the soul and mention the flesh alone? Is it not plain that he exhibited the visible nature and by its means signified the nature united to it? For the mention of the soul is understood of course in that of the flesh. For when we hear the prophet saying "Let all flesh bless His holy name," we do not understand the prophet to be exhorting bodies of flesh without souls, but believe the whole to be summoned to give praise in the summoning of a part.

—Theodoret of Cyrus, *Demonstrations by Syllogisms* 9

Questions to Think About
1. Do I trust in the Lord's mercy enough to turn to him when I know I've sinned?
2. What habits of the heart do I need to cultivate in order to see God's glory in all his works?

About the Fathers

What follows are thumbnail sketches of the Church Fathers who authored the meditations included in this volume. Some of the dates are uncertain but are close enough for simple historical placement.

St. Ambrose of Milan (340–397), like his father before him, was a civil servant of the Roman Empire. The Christian Emperor Valentinian I appointed him consular general over a strategically important area of northern Italy. Ambrose governed from Milan. At the time, the local Christian populace was divided in two: between those who accepted the Catholic faith as expressed in the Council of Nicaea (325), and those who subscribed to the Arian heresy. When the Catholic bishop of Milan died in 374, the Arians sought to have him replaced with one of their own. Riots ensued, and Ambrose arrived to quell the unrest. While he was addressing the crowd, a small child called out "Ambrose for bishop!" And soon the mob—both factions included—took up the chant. Ambrose tried to refuse, but the emperor insisted that he accept the position. And so he did—even though he had not yet been baptized. (In the fourth century, there was a trend to delay baptism till old age, in order to avoid the possibility of post-baptismal sin.) Thus, Ambrose received the sacraments and was ordained all at once. He ruled the Church in Milan wisely, and met regularly with his clergy to exhort them to grow in virtue. He preached brilliantly on the Scriptures, drawing insights from the Christian East. Ambrose also introduced Eastern customs, such as hymn singing, into his Church. The Arians remained a problem, as they enjoyed support from members of the imperial family. But he opposed them with good doctrine and good singing—and he prevailed. A tough negotiator, Ambrose also insisted on the rights of the Church over the intrusions of the emperors. Again, he prevailed, setting an important precedent for bishops down through the ages. He played a key role in the conversion of St. Augustine of Hippo (see below), teaching him the practice of spiritual interpretation of the Old Testament. He also served as spiritual director to Augustine's mother, St. Monica.

St. Aphrahat (c. 270–c. 345), sometimes called Aphraates, is commonly known as the "Persian Sage." He lived in the lands we know today as Iran, Iraq, and Syria. He wrote in Syriac, a dialect of Aramaic, the language spoken by Jesus. Thus he provides evidence of an early Semitic Christianity relatively free of Greek influences and rich in Jewish resonance. About Aphrahat's life we know little for certain, except what we find in his twenty-three brilliant sermons, called *The Demonstrations*. They are thoughtful works of apologetics—defenses of the faith—set down as answers to the inquiries of a friend. *The Demonstrations* show a keen awareness of the arguments against Christianity advanced by the Jewish community of Babylon. Aphrahat was a convert to Christianity, and he lived in a community of celibate men called the Sons of the Covenant. His writings seem to have emerged between the years 337 and 345. According to tradition, he served as a bishop of the Church. Aphrahat had a profound understanding of the Old Testament, as well as then-current Jewish customs and the biblical interpretation of the rabbis. He defended Christian doctrines and practices—such as celibacy, the doctrine of the Real Presence, sacramental confession, and Marian devotion—based largely on the testimony of the Old Testament.

St. Athanasius of Alexandria (c. 293–373) is one of the most important figures in the history of Christian doctrine. As a young deacon, he served as secretary to St. Alexander, the bishop of Alexandria. It was a tumultuous time. With the accession of the Emperor Constantine, Christians were at last free to practice their faith without fear of persecution. But soon the Church "at peace" found itself bitterly divided by a heresy that spread rapidly through the empire. The heresy originated with a priest named Arius in the very city where Athanasius lived. Arius thought that the orthodox doctrines of the Trinity and Incarnation were unreasonable: a father's life, he said, must precede the life of his son; and a son must be dependent upon his father for life. Thus, he denied that Jesus was coeternal and coequal with God the Father. The Arian doctrine won over government officials, many bishops, and entire congregations. Constantine grew alarmed, and he feared that the Christian divisions would threaten the empire's hard-won peace and unity. So he summoned the bishops to a council at Nicaea, near the imperial capital (in modern Turkey). Athanasius attended as the secretary of Alexander, and he helped his bishop formulate the true doctrine with precision and clarity. They coined the phrase that we profess today in the Nicene Creed when we say that God the Son is "consubstantial with the Father." Arius complained that the word was found nowhere in Scripture. But the bishops argued that the idea is implicit in the Scriptures, and they condemned Arius. Alexander died soon after the council, and Athanasius (not yet thirty years old) was chosen as his successor. The young bishop inherited a difficult task, as Arius still had many friends and disciples throughout the world. Arian power waxed and waned as the emperors rose and fell, some orthodox, some heretics. Athanasius was exiled many times; he was tried on trumped-up murder charges; he had to flee assassins on several occasions. Opposed by bureaucrats and fellow bishops, he often had to endure seemingly alone. But even in exile he worked tirelessly. He composed treatises and letters, and traveled so that he could personally lobby the emperor and the pope. Not only was he the great defender of the divinity of Christ, in later years he would produce the first systematic defense of the divinity of the Holy Spirit. He spent most of his last decade restored to his diocese.

St. Augustine of Hippo (354–430) is one of the most influential thinkers in all human history. His influence extends to many fields of endeavor. In literature, he perfected the genres of memoir and autobiography. During his lifetime he was considered one of the top rhetoricians in the world; he is still counted among the great prose stylists in the Latin language. His *City of God* laid the foundation for mainstream political thought for more than a millennium. He was warm, witty, winsome, and a brilliant preacher. He was a prize-winning poet. He wrote an influential set of rules that are still observed in monasteries. He developed definitive refutations of several heresies and helped the Church to welcome home the sheep who had strayed. He was adept at neoplatonic philosophy and demonstrated how it might be used well as a handmaid for Christian theology.

Augustine's life represents a classic form of the conversion story. Born in North Africa to a devout Catholic mother and a pagan father, he fell into mischief and then serious sin. He took up with a concubine and had a son out of wedlock. He achieved great worldly success while dabbling in the esoteric religion of the Manicheans—who preached a spiritual mishmash of Christianity, Buddhism, Judaism, and Zoroastrianism. Through all Augustine's wanderings, his mother, Monica, prayed for him. When he took a teaching position in Rome she followed him there, even though he tried to ditch her by leaving at night. Eventually, both mother and son ended up in Milan, where they were influenced by the bishop St. Ambrose (see above). Ambrose helped Augustine through his remaining difficulties, instructed him, and baptized him. Augustine and some friends—along with his son and his mother—set up a semi-monastic community in northern Italy. After Monica's death, Augustine returned to North Africa, where he was pressed into service of the Church. As bishop, he was involved in many important events, and was active (for example) in the synods that definitively established the canon of the New Testament. He was bishop for thirty-four years. In 430 he fell ill and died as the barbarian Vandals were laying siege to his city.

St. Basil of Caesarea (329–379) is honored as "Basil the Great." He was born into a family rich by worldly standards—and even richer by heavenly measures. His maternal grandfather was a martyr. His paternal grandparents are venerated as confessors who suffered for the faith. Three of his siblings are canonized saints. A bright young man, he studied at schools in Cappadocian Caesarea, Constantinople, and Athens. In Athens he studied with a future emperor, Julian. Through many years of his studies, he was accompanied by his childhood friend, Gregory of Nazianzus. He returned to Caesarea to teach rhetoric, but discerned a call to the contemplative life. Once more, he went abroad, but this time it was to study the various types of monasticism practiced in Syria, Mesopotamia, Palestine, and Egypt. Returning once again to Caesarea, he set up a community on his family estate. Soon he attracted many disciples, including several members of his family. Basil also engaged in the theological controversies of his day, especially against the Arians. He was increasingly drawn into service of the Church, and was ordained to the priesthood in 364 and chosen to be bishop in 370.

As metropolitan of all Cappadocia, Basil was an industrious leader, constantly writing, teaching, and preaching. He wrote one of the earliest doctrinal treatises on the Holy Spirit. He was an active reformer of morals, monastic life, and liturgy. He was a builder, too, constructing a so-called "New City," dedicated to the service of the poor, the sick, and travelers. He died young and was not able to achieve many of his dearest goals, but his influence on the next generation was profound, and every subsequent generation has been indebted to his theology.

St. Clement of Rome (first century) was one of the earliest popes, probably the third after the Apostle Peter. He was a deeply cultured man, well versed in the Scriptures of both Testaments, probably conversant with pagan philosophy, and a master of argument and Greek composition. We possess only one of his works, but it is a very important document: his *Letter to the Corinthians*. Scholars differ now, as they did in the ancient world, on the precise date of the letter, with estimates ranging from AD 67 to AD 95. Clement composed the letter to exhort the Church in Corinth to return to discipline and order. He was fond of the idea of harmony, which he saw exemplified in the laws of nature and in God's ordering of ancient Israel. Clement concluded that God has given the Church a certain harmonious form of hierarchy and a prescribed order of worship. He urged the Corinthians to heal their dissensions and observe the order that was established by the Apostles.

Clement's letter was revered in the Early Church. In some ancient manuscripts, it was included with the canonical books of Scripture. In the Corinthian Church, it was proclaimed in the liturgy as late as the middle of the second century. Catholics have always viewed the letter as a very early witness to Roman and papal authority, since a leader of the Church of Rome was writing to discipline a faraway Church in Greece.

The letter is important for other reasons as well: it demonstrates the early acceptance of many of the genuine books of the New Testament, and it testifies to the martyrdom of Saints Peter and Paul in Rome. According to tradition, the Emperor Trajan banished Clement to work in the mines in lands that are now in the Ukraine. There he continued to evangelize with remarkable success, infuriating his captors. They killed him by binding him to an anchor and casting him into the sea.

St. Cyprian of Carthage (d. 258) was raised in a pagan household in Roman Africa. Trained as a lawyer, he rose to prominence in his profession. Disgusted by corruption in government and immorality in society, he came to admire the Christians of his city, who lived by high moral standards and remained steadfast amid intermittent persecution. He took instruction in the faith and was baptized. The Church put his extraordinary gifts to good use. Eventually he was made bishop of Carthage. When the persecutions intensified, Cyprian went into hiding in order to exercise his ministry more effectively. He wrote many pastoral letters to the "underground" Church. Meanwhile, many Christians died for the faith. Others abandoned the faith in order to save their earthly lives. And still others bribed officials or committed deceptions to evade the executioner. When the persecutions eased up (albeit briefly), the surviving Christians fell to bickering. Those who had withstood torture argued against readmitting the weaker Christians who had committed apostasy. Some argued against forgiveness of those who had practiced evasive tactics as well. Some even opposed Cyprian because he had gone into hiding. Cyprian was the first Christian to think systematically through the theological and pastoral problems that arose because of the persecutions. He was one of the Church's early theologians, and he composed foundational studies in the theology of the sacraments and of the Church. He corresponded with many bishops throughout the world, including the popes who were his contemporaries, many of whom would die as martyrs, as would Cyprian himself.

St. Cyril of Jerusalem (c. 313–386) began his years as bishop under a cloud of suspicion. During the fourth century, the Arian heresy dominated the churches intermittently, as Arian emperors rose and fell. Cyril was appointed to office during an Arian regime, and was consecrated by an Arian bishop. As a result, many faithful churchmen were wary of him; and yet, the Arians knew he was not one of theirs. Thus, he was marginalized by both parties. Indeed, he was exiled from his see three times, and once for eleven years! A local council delegated St. Gregory of Nyssa (see below) to travel to Jerusalem to investigate Cyril. Gregory vindicated Cyril, affirming his fidelity to the true faith. Cyril took part in the Council of Constantinople (380), where again his orthodoxy was confirmed. Cyril is best known for his *Catechetical Lectures*, a series of basic instructions for new converts. In these he provides an in-depth course in Christian doctrine and practice, including the sacraments (especially Baptism, Eucharist, and Confirmation, but also Penance), the moral life, prayer, and a step-by-step guide to the Mass.

Egeria (fourth century, in some manuscripts called *Etheria* and in others *Silvia*) was a wealthy and devout woman from northwestern Spain who made a pilgrimage to the Holy Land, documenting it in detail for the benefit of her religious community back home. As she describes her visits to holy places in Sinai, Judea, and Galilee, she also gives us priceless peeks into monastic life in her times, as well as the observance of the Church calendar and various local liturgical customs. She was a warm writer and keen observer of detail. Other than what we find in her pilgrim journal, we know nothing about her life.

Eusebius of Caesarea (c. 263–339) spent half his life in the persecuted Church and half in the newly triumphant Church. In his youth he was a disciple of St. Pamphilus, who was himself a disciple of Origen (see below). Pamphilus died a martyr, and Eusebius was himself imprisoned for the faith. While his predecessors had a dominant interest in the spiritual and allegorical interpretation of the Bible, Eusebius was most interested in history, which he saw fulfilled in Jesus Christ. He wrote about salvation history as it was recorded in Scripture. He also wrote about the history of pagan philosophical ideas and how even these prefigured Christ.

But he is most famous for his massive *History of the Church*. Eusebius sought to document the story of the faith from the earthly ministry of Christ and the Apostles to the breaking news of his own day. To do so, he drew from the writings of his predecessors, the Early Church Fathers; he traveled to consult the archives in far-flung churches; he conducted interviews; and he drew upon his own memories of discipleship and suffering. In his history he quoted many of these primary sources, sometimes at great length. He even reproduced long lists of bishops who served in the churches founded by the Apostles. These he considered the Church's spiritual genealogy. In many cases, Eusebius's quotations are the only surviving remains of ancient works, the only remaining reports of important events. When Christianity at last was legalized under the Emperor Constantine, Eusebius found favor at the imperial court. He composed panegyrics of praise and a gilded biography of the emperor. In churchly matters, he was at times too willing to compromise doctrine in order to preserve peace. In the Arian controversy, he encouraged Arians and semi-Arians, even after their condemnation by the Council of Nicaea (325). He is considered the father of Church history.

St. Gregory of Nazianzus (329–389), sometimes called "Gregory the Theologian," is one of the three great Cappadocian Fathers (see St. Basil and St. Gregory of Nyssa). After receiving an excellent education, he wished to live a secluded life of prayer and contemplation. But his father, who was bishop of Nazianzus, ordained his son a priest against the young man's will. Gregory panicked and fled to the monastic community of his friend Basil, but Basil sent him back home to resume his priestly duties. Gregory served his father's Church and was eventually named a bishop himself. He worked so hard that after only a few years, his health failed. To recuperate, he spent the next several years studying and praying. From seclusion he became a celebrity. His literary works—poetry, homilies, and theology—earned him an international reputation, and he was summoned to the imperial capital, Constantinople, to serve as its bishop. His congregation in the capital roiled with political intrigue and an array of heresies. His enemies even challenged the validity of Gregory's appointment. He didn't have the stomach for the work needed in the city. So Gregory presided over the watershed Council of Constantinople in 381 and then promptly submitted his resignation. He returned to Nazianzus, where he took up work as his father's successor. After a short time there, he retired, finally, to the seclusion he had so long desired.

St. Gregory of Nyssa (c. 335–c. 395), as younger brother of St. Basil (see above), grew up in a remarkable Christian family. Through his youth he was tutored by his brother Basil and his sister Macrina, and early on he was dedicated to the service of the Church. He abandoned that vocational track, however, to teach rhetoric, and he married a woman named Theosebeia. We do not know whether the marriage ended with her death or whether both spouses decided to dedicate themselves to the celibate life. Gregory was relatively young when his brother Basil consecrated him bishop of a small see. Though Gregory was a great mystic and intellectual, he was no administrator. Even his brother Basil deemed him a failure as a leader. He was inept in financial matters, clueless about Church politics, and a weak disciplinarian. To make matters worse, Arian heretics dominated his region. They had contempt for Gregory and brought him up on charges of financial mismanagement; and while he was away on business, they deposed him. Since the emperor at the time was an Arian, Gregory had no recourse to justice. With the rise of a new emperor, he was able to return, and he was later appointed bishop of the much larger city of Sebaste. In the late fourth century, Gregory won respect as the greatest living theologian. He was a prolific author, and his works include the Church's first catechism, several books on prayer and contemplation, and many ventures in biblical interpretation and speculative theology. Both Church and state considered him an arbiter of orthodoxy. He was a powerful voice for true doctrine at the Council of Constantinople in 381.

Pope St. Gregory the Great (c. 540–604) was born into the old Roman aristocracy, a senatorial family, though his family had been Christian for many generations. On his family tree were two popes before him. In early life, however, Gregory served in civil government. It was a difficult time for Rome. Barbarian incursions into Italy sent a steady stream of refugees into the city. The constant state of war played havoc with commerce and communications as well. Civil order was breaking down. As an aristocrat, Gregory felt a strong obligation to stewardship for the city. He rose to the position of prefect, roughly equivalent to mayor. At the end of his service, he made a radical decision. He divested himself of his wealth; and like St. Basil before him, turned his family estate into a monastery. Deeply influenced by the monastic writings of St. Benedict, he pursued prayerful studies in theology and Scripture. It was not to last. The pope himself summoned Gregory to the service of the Church. He ordained him a deacon and sent him on a diplomatic mission to Constantinople. Gregory remained there for seven years before returning to Rome and a mixed life of contemplation and active service. A flood devastated Rome in 589, followed by a plague in 590, which killed Pope Pelagius. Gregory was chosen as his successor.

Gregory seemed ill-suited to the task. His health was frail, and he was confined to bed much of the time. Yet from his sickbed he carried off one of the most remarkable pontificates in all history! He was a tireless correspondent, and he worked hard to restore discipline to the clergy. He renewed the liturgy, and his ritual legacy remains with us today. He was the first monk to be elected pope, and he was a great promoter of monasticism. Yet he also greatly encouraged missionary work. While civil structures collapsed, he strengthened the authority and pastoral acumen of the Church's bishops, establishing lines of communication and governance that would serve society well into the Middle Ages. He negotiated with the fierce tribes of Lombards and kept them from invading the city. Gregory was, in a sense, the last and greatest of the old Roman nobles; as his old world passed away, he prepared the Church for the new.

St. Hilary of Poitiers (c. 300–368) was born to a pagan family in Gaul (modern France). As a young man, he sought the truth through philosophy. He also married and had a daughter. Eventually his truth-seeking led him to the Catholic faith. He converted and was baptized. It is not clear whether he became a widower at some point or whether he and his wife adopted celibacy by mutual consent. Hilary lived such an exemplary Christian life that he was chosen bishop of Limonum (modern Poitiers). He soon established himself as the Western Church's most articulate defender of the Nicene faith against the Arian heresy. This roused opposition by bishops in his region who favored Arianism—and enjoyed the patronage of the Arian emperor. Hilary was exiled from Gaul to distant Phrygia (in modern Turkey). He used his exile to good effect. He studied theology wherever he went, acquiring a rare mastery not only of the Eastern Fathers but also of the many subtle shadings of contemporary theological speculation. When he composed his greatest work, *On the Trinity*, he incorporated the orthodox heritage, yet found persuasive ways to communicate it clearly to Arians. Hilary also brought home Eastern methods of biblical interpretation, which he famously applied to the psalms and St. Matthew's Gospel. He taught Trinitarian doctrine through hymns as well, some of which, in translation, are still in modern hymnals. He returned to his homeland, where he served several years before his death.

St. Jerome (c. 347–420) was raised in a Christian family in Stridon (in modern Croatia). In his teens he went to Rome for literary studies in the classics, and there he experienced a call to deeper Christian commitment. He and several friends decided to live an ascetical life in common. After a time, Jerome traveled eastward to Syria, for a while settling as a hermit in the desert. He attended the Council of Constantinople (380) as an advisor and then returned to Rome, where he was soon drafted into service as secretary to Pope St. Damasus I. In Rome a growing number of small communities of women were living the religious life. Jerome directed many of them in their piety and studies. After the pope's death, Jerome went east again, and many of those women ascetics followed him. He established monasteries in Bethlehem and set to writing and translating in earnest. He overhauled the popular Latin translation of the Bible (the Vulgate); he even learned Hebrew in order to fine-tune the Old Testament. He wrote voluminously. He is most famous for his biblical commentaries, but he also produced important works combating heresy, letters of spiritual direction, books of apologetics, and the first encyclopedia of Christian biography.

St. John Cassian (c. 370–435) hailed from the region that is now Romania. He was very young when he dedicated himself to God. He traveled with a companion to the Holy Land so that they could enter a monastery. Eventually they settled in Egypt before moving on to Constantinople. There, Cassian was profoundly influenced by the bishop, St. John Chrysostom (see below). When Chrysostom fell afoul of the emperor, Cassian traveled to Rome to appeal the bishop's case before the pope. While in Rome he met and befriended the theologian who would later become Pope St. Leo I. After Chrysostom's demise, Cassian finally settled down in Gaul (modern France), where he founded several monasteries. To educate his monks, he recounted stories of his encounters with the great Fathers of the Egyptian desert. He also preached conferences on the virtues and practices of the spiritual life. These works proved very important in the development of western monasticism—and of Catholic spirituality in general.

St. John Chrysostom (c. 347–407) was raised in Antioch by his widowed mother. He was given the best educational opportunities and studied under the most famous rhetorician of his day. At school, it seemed he was destined to be a civil servant. But with graduation he and a close friend decided to form what was called a "brotherhood"—a household where they could share a common life of voluntary poverty, prayer, and Scripture study. John's mother objected, however, and begged him not to make her "a widow all over again." So he agreed to pursue his life of renunciation at home. Three years later, he managed to break free and join the solitaries in the mountain wilderness. He lived in a cave by himself. He hardly slept at all and he went without protection from the extremes of heat and cold. For hours each day, he read the Scriptures until he had memorized entire books. He continued these austerities even after his health had begun to decline. Only when he needed medical care did he finally return to the city.

Soon the bishop of Antioch pressed him into service. Ordained a deacon, John began to preach, earning him the nickname "Golden Mouth" (Chrysostom). With the hermit's life permanently behind him, he was ordained a priest and soon gave himself entirely to the care of souls. Word of his preaching reached the imperial capital just as its bishop died. Unwilling to be promoted, John was kidnapped by soldiers and transported to his new assignment: bishop of Constantinople, the most prominent see in the East. Almost immediately John established himself as a reformer of the clergy and monasteries. He also showed great concern for the poor. John castigated the rich for using gold-plated commodes while people were starving in the streets. The clergy and monks resisted his efforts, and the rich resented him. Then the imperial family took offense at his sermons and conspired with powerful churchmen to have John deposed. He was banished to a harsh exile but continued to attract disciples. So he was ordered to march, under military guard, to a distant and more isolated place. Already in poor health, he died on the way. John is renowned as one of the greatest orators of ancient times. Thousands of his works have survived.

St. John of Damascus (c. 676–749) grew up in the early Muslim Caliphate. His father had served as chief financial officer for the Caliph. John grew up with the Caliph's son as his playmate. From a captive monk, John received an excellent education in the sciences and liberal arts, which prepared him well to inherit his father's role in the government. Shortly after he took office, however, a controversy arose in the Church. The Byzantine Emperor Leo III, influenced by emerging Islam, forbade the use of sacred images in churches or for private devotion; to carry out his program, he ordered that all existing images be destroyed. Thus, the emperor's followers became known as "iconoclasts"—that is, "picture smashers." Since John lived beyond the jurisdiction of Byzantium, he was able to publish three powerful defenses of the use of devotional images. These tracts soon spread throughout the Christian world and rallied the people. John argued from Scripture and from common sense. His arguments provided the groundwork for the vindication of icons at the Church's Second Council of Nicaea in 787, long after the saint had died. Eventually John retired to a monastery in the Holy Land. He composed many great works on dogma and liturgy and wrote an encyclopedia of heresies as well. Many scholars consider him to be the last of the Eastern Fathers.

St. Macrina the Younger (324–379) was one of the older children in the family of St. Basil and St. Gregory of Nyssa. Well educated and beautiful, she was betrothed at an early age. When she was twelve, her fiancé died, and she dedicated herself to God as a consecrated virgin. Later, with her brother Basil, she founded a contemplative community and attracted many disciples. She was a primary tutor of her much younger brother Gregory. He, in turn, memorialized her by writing a full-scale biography and mentioning her in other works. Gregory portrays her as teaching theology and spirituality up to the very last moment of her life on earth. If she wrote anything, it has not survived.

St. Methodius of Olympus (d. c. 311) was a bishop and a brilliant theologian. In ancient times he was best known for his Scripture commentaries and apologetics aimed at the anti-Christian arguments of prominent pagans. Though early in life he admired Origen (see below), he later became Origen's most vocal critic. Only a few of his works have survived, the most famous being his treatise on virginity, *The Banquet*. He died a martyr.

Origen of Alexandria (c. 185–254) was just a teenager when his father was martyred for the faith, leaving the boy to support the family. Origen was an academic prodigy and easily found work as a tutor. He attracted many students, even as he himself pursued advanced studies in a variety of disciplines. Origen's great love, though, was Scripture, and he communicated this love well to those he taught. When he was in his early twenties, his bishop entrusted him with the instruction of converts. One man he converted—a man of tremendous wealth—was so grateful that he subsidized Origen to employ a staff of secretaries to take dictation and prepare his books for publication. As a result, Origen was able to produce thousands of books in the course of his lifetime. Most were commentaries or homilies on the books of the Bible. Some, however, were treatises on prayer, martyrdom, apologetics, and other occasional topics. He also produced the first critical edition of the Bible, incorporating the original texts and various translations in parallel columns. Because Christians far and wide wished to hear him lecture, he traveled extensively.

Once, while visiting Caesarea in Palestine, the bishops

there forced him to receive holy orders. Origen's own bishop was so infuriated by this that he banished him. Origen then settled in Caesarea, where he reestablished his school and drew many disciples and inquirers. All his life, he hoped to die as a martyr, as his father had. When the persecutions intensified under the Emperor Decius, he was arrested and tortured over the course of many days. But he persevered in the faith and still survived, though enfeebled by the ordeal. He suffered about two more years before dying.

Origen was even more controversial in death than he had been in life. He was among the first speculative theologians, and his speculation sometimes strayed out of bounds in matters that had not yet been clearly defined by the Church. Later councils condemned certain propositions found in Origen's teaching, but these were not his core doctrines, and he always insisted that he wished to be a "man of the Church," faithful to Catholic doctrine. In recent times he has undergone a rehabilitation and has been cited often as an authority in papal encyclicals and in the *Catechism*.

Theodoret (c. 393–457) was the bishop of Cyrus in Syria. His diocese was like a borderland enriched by two cultures—Syrian Greek and Syro-Persian. Theodoret knew the languages and theological traditions of both. Happy with his life as a monk and Scripture scholar, he was summoned to be a bishop and went along dutifully, if grudgingly. Once in office, he excelled at the task, improving not only the spiritual welfare of his congregation, but their material welfare as well. He oversaw the construction of churches, bridges, and aqueducts. During the Nestorian controversy, he found himself caught in the middle of warring factions. He was not an ally of the wayward Nestorius; but neither did he support the particular anti-Nestorian approach taken by St. Cyril of Alexandria. Their differences were surely exacerbated by the perpetual rivalry between the cities of Antioch and Alexandria, and between their schools of theology. Opposing St. Cyril, he was lumped in with the Nestorians and excommunicated, though he was later rehabilitated. As a new heresy, Monophysitism, emerged, Theodoret was invaluable to the Church as it formulated a theological response grounded in the Scriptures. Pope St. Leo the Great addressed him as a "fellow worker." He is the subject of an appreciative biography by Cardinal John Henry Newman.

Sources

The main series of translations from which I've drawn are the Ante-Nicene Fathers (which I've abbreviated in citations as ANF), the Nicene and Post-Nicene Fathers, Series 1 (abbreviated NPNF1), and the Nicene and Post-Nicene Fathers, Series 2 (abbreviated NPNF2). Thus NPNF2 6:122–123 should lead you to volume 6 in the second Post-Nicene series, pages 122 and 123. All three series are available in many places online. You'll find them at www.tertullian.org and www.ccel.org with page numbers intact. They're also at www.NewAdvent.org in plain text. A multivolume reprint edition is available from Hendrickson Publishers, Peabody, Massachusetts.

The English language has undergone great changes in the last hundred and fifty years, so I have adapted the material, translating it from Victorian English to modern English, consulting the Greek or Latin originals whenever possible. The Church Fathers belong to the whole Church and not just to its universities, and I hope my adaptations lead beyond scholarship to a wider devotional readership.

In some cases, I have prepared new translations; these instances are indicated in the notes below. Most of the Greek and Latin sources are in the *Patrologia Graeca* (abbreviated PG) and *Patrologia Latina* (PL).

The Fathers followed the Septuagint Greek Old Testament in its numbering of the Psalms. This differs slightly from most modern Psalters, and so the Fathers' numbering will seem, to some readers, to be off by one. I have tried to note these instances as unobtrusively as possible.

Introduction

St. John Chrysostom. *Exposition of Psalm 41*. New translation from PG 55.155–156.

The Pilgrimage of Etheria. Translated by M.L. McClure and C. L. Feltoe. London: SPCK, 1919. P. 20. Online at http://www.ccel.org/m/mcclure/etheria/etheria.htm.

The Early Christians on the Psalms

St. Jerome. *Commentary on Ephesians*. New translation from PL 26.561–562.

St. Gregory of Nyssa. *Life of St. Macrina*. Translated by W. K. Lowther Clarke. London: SPCK, 1916. Pp. 60–61. Adapted. Online at http://www. tertullian. org/fathers/gregory_macrina_1_life. htm.

St. Athanasius. *Letter to Marcellinus*. In *St. Athanasius: On the Incarnation*. Crestwood, NY: St. Vladimir Seminary Press, 1998, pp. 97, 116.

Psalm 1

St. Basil the Great, *Homily on Psalm 1*. New translation from PG 29.209–213.

Psalm 2

St. Aphrahat. *Demonstration* 17.4–6. NPNF2 13:387–388. Adapted.

St. Augustine. Expositions on the Psalms 2.1, 2.6–7. NPNF1 8:2–3. Adapted.

Psalm 4

St. Gregory of Nazianzus. *Funeral Oration on His Sister Gorgonia*, 22. NPNF2 7:244. Adapted.

Psalm 9

St. Augustine. *On the Holy Trinity* 14.13. NPNF1 3:192. Adapted.

Psalm 12

St. Augustine. *Expositions on the Psalms* 12.6–7. NPNF1 8:44–45. Adapted.

Psalm 15

St. Hilary of Poitiers. *Homilies on the Psalms.* Quoted in Pope John Paul II, General Audience, February 4, 2004. Online at http://www.vatican.va/holy_father/john_paul_ii/audiences/2004/documents/hf_jp-ii_aud_20040204_en.html.

Psalm 19

St. John Chrysostom. *Homiles on Romans* 3.20. NPNF1 11:352. Adapted.

Psalm 22

Eusebius of Caesarea. *Demonstratio Evangelica* 10.8. Translated by W. J. Farrar. London: SPCK, 1920. Pp. 502–503. Adapted. Posted online at: http://www.tertullian.org/fathers/eusebius_de_12_book10.htm.

Psalm 23

St. Cyril of Jerusalem. *Catechetical Lectures* 22.7 (*On the Mysteries* 4.7). NPNF2 7:152. Adapted.

St. Cyril of Jerusalem. *Catechetical Lectures* 1.6. NPNF2 7:7. Adapted.

Psalm 27

Origen. *De Principiis* (Latin edition of Rufinus) 3.2.5. ANF 4:333–334. Adapted.

St. Ambrose. *On Repentance* 1.14.77. NPNF2 10:341–342. Adapted.

Psalm 29

St. Gregory of Nyssa. *On the Baptism of Christ.* NPNF2 5:523. Adapted.

St. Augustine. Expositions on the Psalms 29.8. NPNF1 8:67. Adapted.

Psalm 32

St. Ambrose. *On Repentance* 2.5.35–39. NPNF2 10:350.

Psalm 34

St. Cyril of Jerusalem. *Catechetical Lectures* 23.20–23 (*On the Mysteries* 5.20–23). NPNF2 7:156–157. Adapted.

St. Augustine. *Expositions on the Psalms* 34.11. NPNF1 8:75. Adapted.

St. Augustine. *Expositions on the Psalms* 52.13. NPNF1 8:202. Adapted.

St. Jerome. *Letters* 133.6. NPNF2 6:276. Adapted.

Psalm 40

Eusebius of Caesarea. *Demonstratio Evangelica* 1.10. Pp. 59–61. Adapted. Online at http://www.tertullian.org/fathers/eusebius_de_03_book1.htm.

Psalm 42

St. Augustine. *Expositions on the Psalms* 42.1, 3. NPNF1 8:132–133. Adapted.

Psalm 45

St. Ambrose. *Exposition of the Christian Faith* 1.24–25. NPNF2 10:204–205. Adapted.

Psalm 51

St. Clement of Rome. *Letter to the Corinthians* 17–19. ANF 1:9–10. Adapted.

St. John Chrysostom. *Homilies on First Corinthians* 21.10–11. NPNF1 12:124. Adapted.

St. Augustine. *Expositions on the Psalms* 51.5. NPNF1 8:191. Adapted.

Psalm 53

St. John of Damascus. *Exposition of the Orthodox Faith* 1.3. NPNF2 9:2–3. Adapted.

Psalm 54

St. Hilary of Poitiers. *Homilies on the Psalms* 53.4–5. NPNF2 9:244. Adapted.

Psalm 58

St. Augustine. *Expositions on the Psalms* 58.15. NPNF1 8:235. Adapted.

Psalm 67
St. Cyprian of Carthage. *On the Unity of the Church* 7–8. ANF 5:423–424. Adapted.

Psalm 70
St. John Cassian. *Conferences* 10.10. NPNF2 11:405–407. Adapted.

Psalm 73
St. Jerome. *Letters* 23. NPNF2 6:41–42. Adapted.

Psalm 78
St. Ambrose. *On the Mysteries* 8.48–49. Translated by T. Thompson. London: SPCK, 1919. Pp. 66–67. Adapted.

Psalm 82
St. Augustine. *Expositions on the Psalms* 82. NPNF1 8:395–397. Adapted.

St. Cyril of Jerusalem. *Catechetical Lectures*, Prologue 6. NPNF2 7:2. Adapted.

Psalm 85
St. Augustine. *Expositions on the Psalms* 85.7. NPNF1 8:407. Adapted.

Psalm 94
St. Augustine. *Expositions on the Psalms* 94.1, 3. NPNF1 8:459–460. Adapted.

Psalm 100
St. Methodius of Olympus. *Oration on the Psalms* 1. ANF 6:394. Adapted.

Psalm 102
St. Athanasius. *In Defense of His Flight* 15. NPNF2 4:260. Adapted.

Psalm 104
St. John of Damascus. *Exposition of the Orthodox Faith* 2.3. NPNF2 9:18–20. Adapted.

St. Gregory of Nyssa. *On the Soul and the Resurrection*. NPNF2 5:460. Adapted.

Psalm 110

St. Augustine. *Expositions on the Psalms* 110.1–3. NPNF1 8:541–542. Adapted.

St. Ambrose. *Exposition of the Christian Faith* 2.102–105. NPNF2 10:237–238. Adapted.

Psalm 118

St. Gregory the Great. *The Dialogues* 4.39. Translated by P. W. London: Philip Lee Warner, 1911. Pp. 232–234. Adapted. Online at http://www.tertullian.org/fathers/gregory_04_dialogues_book4.htm#C39.

Psalm 121

St. Augustine. *Expositions on the Psalms* 121.1–3. NPNF1 8:591. Adapted.

Psalm 127

Origen. *De Principiis* (Greek edition) 3.1.18. ANF 4:321–322. Adapted.

Psalm 131

St. Hilary of Poitiers. *Homilies on the Psalms*. NPNF2 9:247–248. Adapted.

Psalm 134

St. Hilary of Poitiers. *Homilies on the Psalms* 134. New translation from *S. Hilarii: Opera Omnia*. Edited by Franciscus Oberthur. Wirceburgi: Libraria Staheliana, 1785. Pp. 150–151.

St. Augustine. Expositions on the Psalms 134.3. NPNF1 8:624. Adapted.

Psalm 137

St. Ambrose. *On Repentance* 2.11.104. NPNF2 10:358. Adapted.

St. Augustine. Expositions on the Psalms 137.13. NPNF1 8:632. Adapted.

Psalm 141

St. Augustine. *Expositions on the Psalms* 141.3–4. NPNF1 8:645. Adapted.

Psalm 145

St. Athanasius. *First Discourse Against the Arians* 4.12. NPNF2 4:313. Adapted.

Theodoret of Cyrus. *Demonstrations by Syllogisms* 9. NPNF2 3:246. Adapted.